Y0-BOJ-823

The WAY for all SEASONS

William Powell Tuck

BROADMAN PRESS
Nashville, Tennessee

© Copyright 1987 ● Broadman Press
All Rights Reserved
4215-41
ISBN: 0-8054-1541-6
Dewey Decimal Classification: 226.93
Subject Heading: Beatitudes
Library of Congress Catalog Number: 87-8008
Printed in the United States of America

Unless otherwise stated, all Scripture quotations are from the Revised Standard
Version of the Bible, copyrighted 1946, 1952, © 1971, 1973.
Scripture quotations marked NEB are from *The New English Bible.* Copyright
© The Delegates of the Oxford University Press and the Syndics of the Cam-
bridge University Press, 1961, 1970. Reprinted by permission.
Scripture quotations marked KJV are from the King James Version of the Bible.
Scripture quotations marked GNB are from the *Good News Bible,* the Bible in
Today's English Version. Old Testament: Copyright © American Bible Society
1976; New Testament: Copyright © American Bible Society 1966, 1971, 1976.
Used by permission.

Library of Congress Cataloging-in-Publication Data

Tuck, William Powell, 1934-
   The way for all seasons.

   1. Beatitudes—Criticism, interpretation, etc.
I. Title.
BT382.T82   1987   226'.9306   87-8008
ISBN 0-8054-1541-6

To Catherine and Bill,
who have brought happiness
to me along the way

Contents

Preface

Mary and John, a bright, attractive young couple, have been married only a few years. They have a lovely baby daughter, a good salary, an expensive home, two fine cars, a color television set, and all the other modern conveniences. Nevertheless, something is missing from their marriage. John and Mary are both unhappy and they do not know why. They know a void exists in their lives, but they would have difficulty acknowledging that their problem is basically a religious one. The problem of this young couple is often tragically the same for many others today.

A middle-aged woman could not hold back the tears as she poured out the story of how her husband of some twenty-five years walked out and left her and her two children for another woman. He said something was missing from his life, and he wanted to find it. He was looking for happiness. A young college student put a gun to his head and pulled the trigger, leaving behind a note declaring, "I can't stand this awful boredom any longer." A young teenager sat in jail weeping with his head in his hands. "I only used the drugs for a quick thrill," he said. "I wanted more excitement in my life." Happiness was also their illusive goal.

The teachings of Jesus, especially as found in the Beatitudes, offer resources which could help each of these and others today to find deeper meaning in life. The teachings in these timeless Beatitudes offer us some challenging guidelines for following Christ in the eighties and in the years to come. The Beatitudes, however, are not merely good advice. They offer the key to authentic living—the key that can unlock the door to genuine happiness.

Most of us judge the significance of our lives in terms of whether or not we are happy. *Happiness,* however, is not an easy word to define. In the 1960s, a popular song expressed the dilemma: Happiness is different things to different people. Many Americans see happiness as an inalienable right and devote much of their energy to the pursuit of happiness as though it could be purchased from a market shelf. Happiness is dangled before us by various advertising media as a lure to entice us into believing that life consists mainly in what we buy, wear, and eat or where we have been, stay, and go. Happiness is depicted in terms of a secure job, a nice home, enough money to buy the comforts and luxuries of life, two cars in the garage, membership in the country club, a good insurance policy, a solid retirement plan, and time for leisure and relaxation at the close of a day's work. Happiness is often measured in terms of financial security, material possessions, and social standing. Ironically, many who have so many things still find they have little for which to live.

The ideas of happiness which Jesus spoke of in the Beatitudes stand in marked contrast to the standards of the world. Our familiarity with the Beatitudes often causes us to lose sight of their radical nature. Some have seen these words as foolish, idealistic, unrealistic, impossible, an interim ethic, or only for a selected few. Although the words were delivered by Jesus so that the crowd may have heard them, they were directed primarily to His disciples. The world at large may find the words of the Beatitudes strange and impossible to achieve. The standards raised in these teachings are not addressed to every person but to those who have already made a commitment of their lives to Christ.

It is difficult for one to attempt to apply the high Christian ideas noted in these teachings without the essential commitment to the Teacher of these principles. Many find it impossible to live by the Beatitudes because they have been unwilling to surrender to the Teacher of them. Christian discipleship is always person centered. In committing our life to the Christlike way we surrender it to a Person, Jesus Christ, and not to principles or codes of conduct. Christ, then, becomes the touchstone and guide for our daily living. His teachings take on new meaning for us because we are seeking to be directed and disciplined by Him. As the apostle Paul wrote: "When anyone is joined to Christ he is a new being: the old is gone, the new has come" (2 Cor. 5:17, GNB).

Seldom does the world proclaim the "blessedness" or "happiness" of the poor in spirit, the mourners, the meek, those longing after righteousness, the merciful, or the peacemakers. Modern society seems to herald that blessed are the rich, the powerful, the fashionable, the successful, the strong, the bold, the popular, the pushers, the military and industrial leaders, the hard, the tough, and those on the way up. To many, the ideas of happiness which Jesus taught sound foolish, and they always will until one is able to realize the reality of His deeper insights into the authentic meaning of life. Although the teachings of Jesus may not always appear attractive, the alternative has led not to happiness but selfishness, greed, cruelty, and often destruction. The way of Jesus is a call to a higher way. It is not an easier way but the higher, truer way that leads to genuine abundant living. If taken seriously by Christians, the words in the Beatitudes of Jesus would create a revolutionary change in our style and manner of living.

Long before Christians were called by that name they were spoken of as followers of "the way" or "the road."

By this designation, the early Christians sought to show that they were following Jesus and the way He had lived and traveled. This "way," of course, was the way of the cross. His followers lived daily with the awareness of the words of Christ, "He who does not take his cross and follow me is not worthy of me" (Matt. 10:38). The summons from the Master Teacher is still to come walk in the way. "We must be men of the way," Leslie Weatherhead has observed, "until, while men are too reticent to say so, they may know in their hearts that we have a secret, the clue to life's meaning and purpose and joy, and turn and find their way to his feet."[1] For those who are willing to walk in it, the way of Christ offers direction, meaning, and genuine happiness. The Beatitudes of Jesus provide light along the path of life as we seek to walk in His way. "As ye have therefore received Christ Jesus the Lord, so walk ye in him" (Col. 2:6 KJV). "Walk in the light, as he is in the light" (1 John 1:7 KJV).

I want to express my appreciation to Dr. Frank Stagg, professor emeritus of New Testament Interpretation, The Southern Baptist Theological Seminary, Louisville, Kentucky, for reading the manuscript and offering me the benefit of his critical counsel. I am indebted to Miss Joann Feazell for her kindness in the typing and retyping of the manuscript, and to the Office Services of The Southern Baptist Theological Seminary. Unless indicated otherwise, the Scripture selections are taken from the *Revised Standard Version of the Bible*, copyrighted 1952 and 1971.

Note

1. Leslie D. Weatherhead, *Over His Signature* (New York: Abingdon Press, 1955), p. 103.

The Way for All Seasons

How much such a purpose can mean is well illustrated in the life of Dr. F. W. Boatwright, who served more than half a century as president of the University of Richmond. One day I asked him the secret of his life and he told me this remarkable story. When just a boy he fell into a mill-race, was carried by the water through an underground channel, and later picked up and pronounced dead from drowning. But he had really only been stunned and that night as the family was making arrangements for the funeral he recovered consciousness and lived. He grew up with the firm conviction that he had been miraculously spared for some worthy purpose, and he gave himself with such utter devotion to Christian education that a great university stands today as a living memorial to his determination to make the most of his life.

When I asked him about his philosophy of life he said it was summed up in two sentences: "The greatest use you can make of life is to spend it for something that will outlast it," and "Whatsoever ye do, do it heartily, as to the Lord . . . for ye serve the Lord Christ."

—Theodore F. Adams, *Making the Most of What Life Brings.*

1

Spiritual Poverty

Blessed are the poor in spirit, for theirs is the kingdom of heaven (Matt. 5:3).

Dag Hammarskjöld, secretary-general of the United Nations, died in an air crash on September 18, 1961, in Zambia, Central Africa, while flying there in an attempt to negotiate a cease-fire between United Nations and Katanga rebel forces. E. Stanley Jones told how he had flown over the spot where Hammarskjöld met his tragic death. The pilot of the plane carrying Jones lived in Zambia and told the famous missionary that in the wreckage of the U. N. plane an open map of Nadolo, a town near Leopoldville, Congo, (now Kinshasha, Zaire) was discovered instead of a map of the city of Nadola, Zambia, which was their destination. The pilot had crashed his plane in an open field at night thinking he was at Nadola which had a thousand feet more of landing strip than did Nadolo.

He had followed the wrong map, and the difference between an *o* and an *a* made the difference between life and death. "If you have the wrong mental map of yourself," observed Jones, "you will probably come to wrong landings, a disaster instead of a destination."[1] "I cannot go down any road on anything with anybody who has problems without running straight into the necessity of self-surrender," he continued. "All else is marginal, this is central. I have only one remedy, for I find only one disease —self at the center, self trying to be God."[2]

Jesus knew that each person had to begin with the central problem of his life if he or she wanted to have a meaningful life. Each of us has to learn to love and depreciate one's self, accept and surrender one's self, affirm and deny one's self. The paradoxical understanding of self is not a lesson easily learned or eagerly sought, but it is the beginning point where Jesus initiates the Sermon on the Mount when He declared, "Happy are those who know they are spiritually poor; the Kingdom of heaven belongs to them" (Matt. 5:3, GNB)!

I read about a young mother who was in a line of prisoners to be executed by Nazi soldiers during the Second World War. She refused to give up her baby even when she was beaten mercilessly. A young Christian woman standing near by watched until the guard turned his back and then she quickly pushed the mother out of the line and quietly took her place to be executed. An agnostic, who knew this woman and saw what she had done, declared, "If this is what the Christian faith does, then, I will be a Christian."

This kind of selfless love, however, is not always evident even in Christian circles, but it is the kind of revolutionary self-love which has been revealed to us by God Himself through His Son. We are a puzzle to ourselves and often follow the wrong map for meaningful living. In this Beatitude Jesus offers us guidance for understanding who this "I-me" is and how it can live responsibly with the "you-they" around us. Facing self is life's emerging point of departure where each one of us confronts reality and decides his or her pathway.

Not Self-Depreciation

The poverty of spirit which Jesus indicates as blessed is not to be identified with an attitude of self-depreciation. To look down on one's self or to feel unworthy compared to others is not the intent of this Beatitude. This has often been the image given by much of society when it refers to Christian humility. This kind of humility depicts a Christian as a person who is afraid of life, walked over by others, without the backbone to meet any obstacle, unable to stand up for his own rights, lacking the red blood of courage, standing spineless and helpless, hiding feelings of self-disgust, being used as society's doormat, and defeated and beaten down by the circumstances and demands of life.

If this is what Jesus meant by "poor in spirit," no wonder many reject this dejected picture of a sort of crawling, cowardly, discouraged wormlike creature. Christian humility must convey more of an image of life than a drooping flower after it has been frostbitten. But who says one must accept this distorted misconception of the image of what Jesus means by the "poor in spirit"?

When I was in Richmond, Virginia, recently I noticed a statue of the famous general, Stonewall Jackson. He has always been one of my favorite figures from the Civil War. On one occasion when General Jackson was making preparations to begin a campaign in the Shenandoah Valley, one of his subordinate officers approached him and said, "General Jackson, I'm afraid. I fear that this is an improper deployment of our troops. I'm afraid our strategy is not sound. I'm afraid we're going to lose a lot of men." "Soldier," Jackson replied, as he put his hand on the officer's shoulder, "Never take counsel of your fears." Our fearful, doubtful attitude often reproduces itself in our actions. If we take counsel with our fears, see ourselves as inferior, focus on our failures, dwell on our weaknesses, linger over our limitations, harbor doubts about ourselves, and anticipate defeats, then our worst fears are often realized. This is not what Jesus intended in His concept of the "poor in spirit."

I remember well a former church member into whose home my wife and I were invited on several occasions. Although the table was most attractively done and the meal delicious, she was constantly apologizing for the way the table was arranged, the manner in which the food was prepared, and the way she looked. For some strange reason she felt that she needed to depreciate herself and her work to be appreciated by us.

When I was in college, I had a friend who was an excellent student and a most attractive fellow. Although he had great potential, he was never able to realize it because he was constantly putting himself down and complaining that he could not do the assignments, pass the test, or be acceptable socially with the campus young ladies. His worst fears came to pass, not so much because of lack of ability or intelligence or social grace, but simply through daily self-depreciation.

For some persons the difficulty with themselves is not an image that is too great but one which is too small. Self-conceit is not their albatross. They struggle with a low sense of self-esteem. Their self-image rings hollow and untrue. The projection of their personality is faded and pale.

Instead of being aggressive, they feel beat upon and beseiged. Instead of seeing an image of themselves as strong and vigorous, their reflection appears weak and insipid. They long to be more, but feel they can only be less. They want to take risks in their work and behavior, but their conversations echo faintly in the office and their lives reflect a dim shadow of what they want to do.

They reach out but they feel they cannot really touch. They hunger for acceptance of themselves but cannot really accept themselves much less others. Rather than putting the best foot forward, they constantly think they are marching in reverse. Instead of having an iron fist in working with others, they consider their skills soft and inadequate. Many are bitterly disappointed with themselves and their roles in life.

Broken inside by a lack of self-esteem, many feel they are nobody. "I've never had a break," says one. "I hate to get up in the morning," says another. "I can't face myself," a weary voice exclaims, "so I turned to drink." The hero within gives way to the waging forces without. Their real self has not been attained and may not be. They have given way to a small, weak image instead of the full, complete person they could be.

Several years ago, I was attending a conference in a large city and stopped by to visit with a friend. As I was leaving, I was introduced to a couple who had also come by to say hello while they were in town. After only a few minutes conversation, this new acquaintance said to me, "Why do you put yourself down? Are you aware that in only a few moments you have expressed negative thoughts about yourself?" I had only done it in a joking fashion, I thought, but as I reflected on my conversation with this woman, she was right. I began to ask myself why I had chosen this manner to meet total strangers. Look at the image of myself I had unveiled to this new couple. Sometimes in a type of pseudo-modesty wrapped in a strange type of degrading humor we disclose a weak self-image to others. What we reveal is not a humble spirit but one that is weak and insecure.

The image we have of ourselves often determines what we become. If we view ourselves with a low self-image, that is the way we develop. If we have a healthy view of ourselves, then we will have a positive image. To feel good about one's self is not always a sign of haughtiness or pride but may be a perception which reveals inner security and self-confidence.

We often treat other people harshly, or we are rude, or

we disappoint them, or hurt them not because we are tough, secure, or in control but due to our low self-image and inadequacy. Our actions stem from inferiority, not self-reliance.

The inner man or inner woman has frequently been determined by a misshapened image. To achieve its true potential the inner person needs an image that can lift it to the heights it was created to realize. Most of us live out our lives with limited, broken, or distorted visions of what we could be.

To realize its full potential our self-image needs to be awakened, refocused, and redirected. This is not achieved by our own initiative but by an inner vision of one's higher self. Many of us measure ourselves by our lower self instead of the higher potential self we are created to be. We settle for less when we could be much more. We accept an inferior self instead of a confident image. Why do we assent to an incomplete conception when the possibility for a much greater perception is possible?

I remember reading about a stranger who moved into a new community and began to practice law. Soon he had immersed himself in his legal practice. Sometimes he could be seen walking in the evenings, always alone with his head down and a look of mental distress upon his face. He confessed one day to an artist friend that he had made a sad and terrible mistake in his life. His artist friend did not comment about this but went back to his studio and set to work. Later he invited the melancholy lawyer to view a portrait that he had just completed which he felt was his masterpiece. Surprised and pleased that his judgment should be desired by the artist, he was even more surprised to discover that it was portrait of himself. In the painting, however, he stood erect, with his shoulders thrown back and his head up. Ambition, desire, and hope were written on his face. He studied it in silence for a few moments and then said, "If he sees that in me, then I can see it. If he thinks I can be that, then I can be that man; and what is more, I will be."

Jesus Christ saw into the lives of men and women as no one else ever had. In the eyes of a denying Peter, He saw a rocklike faith. In the countenance of the tax-collector, Matthew, He envisioned a potential disciple of unusual worth. In a thieving Zacchaeus, He saw a beneficent follower. In the persecutor Saul He saw Paul, militant missionary to the Gentiles. In the tear-stained face of Mary Magdalene, He saw a loyal, pure faith. In learned Nicodemus, He foresaw a dedicated, born-anew teacher. In the rich young ruler, He envisioned a committed disciple. In the Samaritan woman at the well, He saw one seeking to reach beyond her frustrated life. In the doubting questions of Thomas, He saw an adventurous faith. Jesus Christ saw, as no other person was able to see, what the lives of the lowest or the best, the most common or most exalted, or even the most rejected could be. He is still seeing that as He looks into our lives today and challenges us to become the higher self which we have been created to be.

In the Great Commandment, Jesus said that " 'you shall love the Lord your God with all your heart, and with all your soul, and with all your mind, and with all your strength.' The second is this, 'You shall love your neighbor as yourself.' There is no other commandment greater than these" (Mark 12:30-31). Here, rather than telling a person to despise himself, Jesus is commanding us to love our neighbors with the same kind of love that we reserve for ourselves. Selfishness is, without question, humanity's basic sin. But healthy self-love is radically different from selfishness. Selfishness sees life from the perspective of self-centeredness and ego satisfaction. One is intent only on what life can do to meet one's own needs. This kind of pride runs counter to the teachings of Jesus because it limits a person's perspective.

On the other hand, a healthy self-love is an acknowledgement that the Christian is aware that God expects His children to have a mature self-image because of His creative and redeeming love (Mark 12:30-31). Pride and narcissism are repulsive and only hinder Christian growth, but a sense of personal worth is appropriate for anyone who is a child of God. This spirit is reflected in the words of the character, Noah, in the black-culture play, *Green Pastures*, "I ain't very much, but I'se all I got." Without an awareness that humanity is a creation of God, we may feel unworthy, but Christian humility is the recognition of humanity's true worth as persons under God. The psalmist reminded us of our significance when he asked and declared:

> What is man that thou art mindful of him,
> and the son of man that thou dost care for him?
> Yet thou hast made him little less than God,
> and dost crown him with glory and honor.
> Thou hast given him dominion over the works of thy hands;
> thou hast put all things under his feet (Ps. 8:4-6).

There is an old story about a housewife who asked the grocery boy his name one day as he delivered the groceries. "Humphrey Bogart," was his reply. "That's a pretty well-known name," the housewife responded. "Well, it ought to be," the boy readily agreed, "I've been delivering groceries in this neighborhood for four years." Every name is significant, particularly if it is our name. Each one of us is unique and important. When we finally arrive at this insight, we have glimpsed something of the worth and significance of our own self.

To love yourself in the biblical sense is to see yourself

in the light of God's love. The gift of life which God has given to every person challenges us to handle it with the respect and high value which he placed on it by his act of creative love. A small boy from a slum area carried a sign which he had made in Vacation Bible School that expresses this truth well; "I'm Me," the sign read. "And that's OK; 'cause God don't make no junk." He was right. The Christian is called in Jesus Christ to a high opinion of himself or herself. The good news of the gospel presents persons as of indescribable worth to God and themselves. Those who are the poor in spirit are humble but not humilitated, self-respecting but not self-centered, self-loving but not selfish, aware of their own value but not egotistical, and self-giving without being self-serving.

Frank Court has told about a college friend of his who had a type of muscle paralysis. The friend decided to sell books one summer. He began by calling at the home of the college president. The president's wife told him that they did not need any books, but, as he was turning to leave, she saw a limp in his walk and exclaimed, "Oh, I am so sorry! I did not know you were lame." The young student, who did not want pity, bristled all over. The president's wife, aware that she had said the wrong thing, quickly added, "I did not mean to imply anything except admiration, but doesn't being lame rather color your life?" "Yes," he responded, "but thank God I can choose the color." So we can choose. We can choose to see ourselves as inferior, inadequate, subordinate, minor, mediocre, deficient, or paltry. On the other hand, we can choose to see ourselves by God's grace as valuable, competent, worthy, adequate, useful, able, and profitable.

The "poor in spirit" have a sense of their own value as children of God and, therefore, are committed to growing deeper in the awareness of what this love is. Without question it involves an awareness of sinfulness and weaknesses, limitations and imperfections, but God's love also calls us to possibilities and potential, creativities, and gifts. Shakespeare focused on a biblical insight when he declared, "Self-love, my liege, is not so vile a sin as self-neglecting."[3] Unless a person respects himself or herself, he or she is unlikely to achieve any worthy goals in life. If you cannot really love yourself, how can you hope to love another?

Spiritual Poverty

It is possible for one to think too lightly of one's own significance. Sometimes that is a problem. On the other hand, our basic problem seldom seems to be thinking too little of ourselves but too highly. Pride has been labeled the root of all sin by most theologians. They seem united in their chorus. "Pride," Pascal observed, "is essentially unjust in that it makes self the center of everything, and it is troublesome to others in that it seeks to make them servient."[4]

Pride has been seen as humanity's basic sin because it reveals our rebellion and defiance against God. "The deepest root of sin therefore is not the senses," said Emil Brunner, "they are, at most occasions of sin—but the spiritual defiance of one who understands freedom as independence, and thus only regards himself as free when he 'feels that he owes his existence to himself alone. . . .' Sin is emancipation from God, giving up the attitude of dependence, in order to try to win full independence, which makes man equal with God."[5] The English theologian J. S. Whale has observed that "The essence of sin is man's self-centered denial of his distinctive endowment. Its final ground is pride which rebels against God and repudiates his purpose. Its active manifestation is self-love. . . ."[6] "Sin means going astray, failing to find the source of life in our search for life," according to the German theologian

Wolfhart Pannenberg. "The going astray consists in every man's striving for the fulfillment of life through enrichment of his own ego, separated from others and from God."7 "The Genesis story of the Fall," declared New Testament scholar Frank Stagg, "is the story of man's revolt against his creature status and his attempt to be like God—to be complete in himself. It is the story of man's self-love, self-trust, and self-assertion."8

In one of William Saroyan's stories there is an old man who has only one string left on his cello. From morning until night, day after day, hour after hour, he played only on that one string. When his patient wife timidly pointed out that other cellists changed their fingers up and down as they played, moving from one position to another, the old man looked at her with a smile and replied: "I might have expected that from you. Your hair is long, but your understanding is short. Of course other players keep moving their fingers. They are trying to find the right place. I have found it!"

Echoes of this same self-centeredness can be heard in the words of one of the characters of Somerset Maugham in *Of Human Bondage*. "The terms vice and virtue have no signification for me," Crenshaw said. "I do not confer praise or blame: I accept. I am the measure of all things, I am the centre of the world." "But there are one or two other people in the world," objected Philip. "I speak only for myself," continued Crenshaw. "I know them only as they limit my activities."9

G. K. Chesterton must have heard a similar declaration himself once and attempted to discount it in the following manner:

> Pride consists in a man making his personality the only test, instead of making the truth the test. It is not pride to wish to do well, or even to look well, according to a real

test. It is pride to think a thing looks ill, because it does not look like something characteristic of oneself. Now in the general clouding of clear and abstract standards, there is a real tendency today for a young man (and even possibly a young woman) to fall back on that personal test, simply for lack of any trustworthy impersonal test. No standard being sufficiently secure for the self to be moulded to suit it, all standards may be moulded to suit the self. But the self as a self is a very small thing and something very like an accident. Hence arises a new kind of narrowness; which exists especially in those who boast of breadth. The skeptic feels himself too large to measure life by the largest things; and ends by measuring it by the smallest thing of all.[10]

In his picturesque way Charles Schulz has given us an image of modern human pride in his "Peanuts" comic strip. Linus is sitting in front of the TV when Lucy comes in and yells, "I don't wanna watch that program. I wanna watch *my* program!" Walking away Linus says, "All right, I'll go upstairs and listen to the radio." While Linus is listening to his radio, Lucy bursts in again and cries, "I don't wanna listen to that program. . . . I wanna listen to *my* program!" Again Linus leaves and responds, "All right, . . . I'll go in the next room and play a few records." This time Lucy stomps in and declares loudly. "I don't wanna listen to those records. . . . I wanna listen to *my* records." Getting up and moving outside, Linus replies, "All right, I'll go outside and look at the stars for a while. . . ." Running up to Linus while he is peering into the night sky, Lucy retorts, "I don't wanna look at these stars. . . . I wanna look at *my*. . . ." Then she pauses without saying a word and finally sighs and walks away.[11]

Pride always asserts itself. It always demands that its own rights and needs be satisfied, often even at the expense or inconvenience of others. What I want, when I want it, is the important matter. The wants or needs of others are not important when a life is utterly selfish. Pride is the excessive love of self to such a degree that one attempts to assume the role of God. Human beings, the created, strive to usurp the role of the Creator. Pride reflects the universal human rebellion against our own limitations as a creature. Direction and meaning are missing from our lives when they are focused inwardly only upon ourselves.

I read about a strange plant in South America which exists by finding a moist place, resting in it for a while sending its roots down and becoming green. However, when this small piece of earth dries up, the plant draws itself together and is blown along by the wind until it finds another moist spot where it repeats the same kind of existence. Throughout its life it continues to roll one place and then another, stopping wherever it finds some water and remaining until the supply is gone. At the end of its journeying, this plant is still nothing but a bundle of dead roots and leaves. The tragedy of many lives is that they only live selfishly off of others as they journey through life. They draw all they can out of someone else's life and move on. They contribute little but demand much; they give sparingly but take all they can; seldom extend their hands to help but continuously expect support from others.

Few persons have admitted their rebellion against God as frankly as Friedrich Nietzsche. One can almost see him shaking his fist against heaven and sense his refusal to accept the notion of anyone higher then himself as he cries:

> Once did people say God, when they looked out upon distant seas; now, however have I taught you to say, Superman. . . . And what ye have called the world shall but be created by you: your reason, your likeness, your will, your

love, shall itself become! And verily, for your bliss, ye discerning ones! . . .

But that I may reveal my heart entirely unto you, my friends: *if* there were Gods, how could I endure it to be no God! *Therefore,* there are no gods.[12]

Within all of us is the false notion of the "superman" who acknowledges no God but himself, who worships at no shrine but his own intellect, and bows at no altar but his own desires. This is humanity's fundamental rebellion against God. In his classic book on the Beatitudes Ralph Sockman listed four adverse effects of the sin of pride: Pride shutters the mind, locks the heart, weakens the hand, and corrupts the conscience.[13] Reinhold Niebuhr, the American theologian, once wrote that humanity's basic sin is our "God Almightyness." "The sin of man is that he seeks to make himself God."[14] The feelings of self-sufficiency, self-centeredness, self-exaltation, self-pleasing, and other forms of pride, continue to block any meaningful relationship to God. Jesus' words, "Blessed are the poor in spirit," became a "stop sign" in our path to bring us to a halt in our drive for self-assertion. The Beatitudes seek to redirect our thinking toward an awareness of our own sinfulness and the absolute dependence we have upon God for release and forgiveness.

If pride is the root of all sin, then poverty of spirit is the foundation on which all the others are built. In Dante's *Divine Comedy* pride is placed on the lowest terrace and when the pride mark is erased from the poet's forehead he hears the angelic choir chanting the Beatitude: "Blessed are the poor in spirit."[15]

Jesus was selective in His choice of placing this Beatitude first. He saw poverty of the spirit as the key to discipleship. As D. Martyn Lloyd-Jones has observed, "There is no one in the Kingdom of God who is not *poor in spirit.*

It is the fundamental characteristic of the Christian and of the citizen of the kingdom of heaven, and all the other characteristics are in a sense the result of this one."[16] This Beatitude in a theological form, according to Lloyd-Jones, is a perfect statement of the doctrine of justification by faith only. Without an awareness of personal sin and the reality of forgiveness, no one can be related properly to God. Genuine happiness can be attained only when one has put himself in proper relationship to the source of all ultimate happiness—God.

In the Old Testament "the poor" often refers to those who "wait on God" (Ps. 10:2; 40:17). The poor are those who are aware of their absolute dependence upon God. To have poverty of the spirit is to be awakened to the reality that although one might possess many things without God all of these things do not count for anything. This poverty makes one wealthy when he or she realizes that the greatest riches are found in a proper relationship to God, who is the source of all things. Those who are the poor in spirit have been emptied of vain pride in the presence of God's holiness and have sensed their dependence upon Him, and are therefore open and receptive to learn and grow spiritually.

The paradox of the Christian gospel is noted in this Beatitude. We receive independence only by becoming dependent, victory only by surrender. We receive only by giving, find only by losing, gain spiritual riches only by acknowledging our spiritual poverty. Jesus said, "If the Son makes you free, you will be free indeed" (John 8:36). In the freedom of discipleship and commitment to Jesus Christ as Lord, one receives not the license to do as one pleases without restriction or restraint but a freedom which challenges one to seek a higher way—the rule of God within one's own life. Without this rule in our life, chaos and division soon control us.

The Rule of God

"Blessed are the poor in spirit; for theirs is the kingdom of heaven." The kingdom of heaven sounds so remote, so distant, so unworldly, so futuristic, so out of touch with contemporary society. The kingdom Jesus refers to here is not so much a geographical location, a plot of land, or a piece of celestial real estate, as it is a reference to the exercise of authority and power. The term *heaven* in New Testament usage was the place where God lived but also came to mean God Himself. Just as we sometimes say in a slang way, "heaven help us," we really mean "God help us." The "kingdom of heaven" which the poor in spirit receive, then, is the rule, power, and guidance of God in their lives here in this present life. The verb points not to the future but to the present. Jesus said the kingdom of heaven *is* ours now, not just *shall be* sometime in the distant future.

When Jesus tells us that "Blessed are the poor in spirit, for theirs is the kingdom of heaven," He is saying in modern language "Happy are those who have emptied themselves of vain pride in the awareness of their own inadequacy and sin and have humbly accepted the rule and power of God in their own life." The presence and power of God become present possessions which reach into eternity, because now God has been made the center of one's life. The rule or power of God comes into a life when the person is willing to "Seek first the kingdom of God." Self is no longer sovereign in one's heart but God is given the guiding hand. Jesus called poverty of the spirit "humility" and indicated it was attained by becoming childlike. In the midst of His teaching, Jesus once stopped and took a child and said to His disciples: "Unless you turn and become like children, you will never enter the kingdom of heaven. Whoever humbles himself like this child,

. . . is the greatest in the kingdom of heaven" (Matt. 18:3-
4). In innocence, dependence, acceptance, and openness,
a child looks to his parents to fulfill his needs. In the same
manner the poor in spirit look to God to fulfill their lives
as they have emptied them of self and opened them to be
filled with the Spirit of God. Real happiness is realized
when the kingdom of self has been replaced by the kingdom of God.

Reaching for Fulfillment

The poverty of spirit which Jesus offers us stands in
sharp contrast to modern human understanding of happiness. Nevertheless, it alone brings inner satisfaction which
is not dependent upon external conditions and possessions. In this Beatitude Jesus has not directed us to think
less of ourselves as persons but He is challenging us to
realize the potential of what we can become when we
have emptied our lives of the destructive force of self-
centeredness and filled our lives instead with His power
and love. This change comes about only as we are aware
of our absolute dependency upon God and give Him full
control of our lives. As we surrender our lives to God we
find genuine victory and happiness. When our life is controlled by God's love, we have immediate possession of
His kingdom because He is now the central force in our
lives. How can we reach this standard?

First, *we must face ourselves*. This Beatitude, Lloyd-
Jones reminded us, really means an emptying while the
others are descriptions of a fullness. "We cannot be filled
until we are first empty."[17] No container can hold more
until its contents have been emptied to make room for
more. The tragedy of self-centeredness is vividly described in Ibsen's drama *Peer Gynt*. At an asylum for the
mentally ill, the superintendent observes:

It's here that men are most themselves—themselves and
nothing but themselves—sailing with outspread sails of
self. Each shuts himself in a cask of self, the cask stopped
with a bung of self and seasoned in a well of self. None has
a tear for others' woes or cares what any other thinks.
. . . Now surely you'll say that he's himself! He's full of
himself and nothing else; himself in every word he says—
himself when he's beside himself.[18]

Our basic sin of pride must be emptied from our life if
Jesus Christ is to direct it now. We are aware that we
cannot throw off the power of selfishness by our own
strength. Paul, conscious of the awesome power of the sin
of pride, cried: "Who will deliver me from this . . . death?"
His answer rings back for himself and us, "Thanks be to
God through Jesus Christ our Lord! For the law of the
Spirit of life in Christ Jesus has set me free from the law
of sin and death" (Rom. 7:24b-25; 8:2). Change can only
come into a life where one has admitted his need and
turned from sin toward God. The New Testament describes this call to turn as repentance, and the act of turning to God itself is depicted as the "new birth" or the
"new creation."

Secondly, *we must face God.* We empty ourselves not
to remain empty but to fill our lives with the presence of
God. The poor in spirit have turned from innate selfishness to find a higher way of service and love—the way of
Christ. Our standard is no longer to measure all things
selfishly by ourselves but to gauge our living by something
higher. "The true way to be humble," Phillips Brooks
once said, "is not to stoop until you are smaller than yourself, but to stand at your real height against some higher
nature that will show you what the real smallness of your
greatness is." When we turn and face God we are confronted by *the* standard and then we understand the
blessedness of the poor in spirit.

I recently had an opportunity of seeing the famous statue of Jesus by the artist Thorwaldsen in Copenhagen. An accident occurred when the statue was being moved and the head of Jesus was bent forward. The only way you can see directly into the eyes and face of Jesus on this statue is to get down on your knees before Him. The redemption Jesus is seeking to bring into our life can be received only by those who are willing to acknowledge humbly that they are poor in spirit. When we begin with this declaration and follow Christ, we sense that we have begun to walk in the only path that brings genuine happiness.

Notes

1. E. Stanley Jones, *Victory Through Surrender* (New York: Abingdon Press, 1966), pp. 8-9.
2. Ibid., p. 14.
3. William Shakespeare, *King Henry V*, Act II, Scene 4.
4. Blaise Pascal, *Faugère*, Vol. I, p. 197.
5. Emil Brunner, *The Christian Doctrine of Creation and Redemption*, vol. II, translated by Olive Wyon (London: Lutterworth Press, 1955), p. 93.
6. J. S. Whale, *Christian Doctrine* (London: Fontana Books, 1958), p. 42.
7. Wolfhart Pannenberg, *The Apostle's Creed*, translated by Margaret Kohl (Philadelphia: The Westminster Press, 1972), p. 164.
8. Frank Stagg, *New Testament Theology* (Nashville: Broadman Press, 1962), p. 19.
9. Somerset Maugham, *Of Human Bondage* (Garden City, N.Y.: Doubleday & Co., Inc., 1936), p. 190.
10. G. K. Chesterton, *The Common Man* (New York: Sheed and Ward, 1950), p. 254.
11. Charles Schulz, *Peanuts*, United Feature Syndicate, Inc., 1966.
12. Friedrich Nietzsche, *Thus Spake Zarathustra*, translated by Thomas Common (New York: The Modern Library, n.d.), pp. 90-91.
13. Ralph Sockman, *The Higher Happiness* (New York: Abingdon-Cokesbury Press, 1950), p. 25f.
14. Reinhold Niebuhr, *The Nature and Destiny of Man* (New York: Charles Scribner's Sons, 1949), p. 140.
15. *The Divine Comedy of Dante Alighieri*, translated by Charles Eliot Norton (Boston: Houghton Mifflin Co., 1920), Book II, Canto XII, vv. 100-114, pp. 92-93.

16. D. Martyn Lloyd-Jones, *Studies in the Sermon on the Mount* (Grand Rapids, Mich.: Wm. B. Eerdmans Publishing Co., 1971), p. 42.

17. Ibid.

18. *Eleven Plays of Henrik Ibsen* (New York: The Modern Library, n.d.), pp. 436-438.

I do not understand this life of ours. But still less can I comprehend how people in trouble and loss and bereavement can fling away peevishly from the Christian faith. In God's name, fling to what? Have we not lost enough without losing that too? If Christ is right—if, as He says, there are somehow, hidden away from our eyes as yet, still there, wisdom and planning and kindness and love in these dark dispensations—then we can see them through. But if Christ was wrong, and all that is not so; if God set His foot on my home crudely, heedlessly, blunderingly, blindly, as I unawares might tread upon some insect in my path, have I not the right to be angry and sore?

If Christ was right, and immortality and the dear hopes of which He speaks do really lie a little way ahead, we can manage to make our way to them. But if it is not so, if it is all over, if there is nothing more, how dark the darkness grows! You people in the sunshine may believe the faith, but we in the shadow must believe it. We have nothing else.

—Arthur John Gossip, *The Hero in Thy Soul.*

2

The Strange Happiness of Grief

Blessed are those who mourn, for they shall be comforted (Matt. 5:4).

A few years ago two English explorers discovered a tomb in Egypt where four thousand years ago a little daughter was laid lovingly to rest in a carved sarcophagus by grieving parents. On the sarcophagus were inscribed the words, "O my life, my love, my little one! Would God I had died for you!" Down through the centuries and out of the blazing desert comes the ancient, yet ever-present, agony of grief. As far back as humanity has recorded history, there is the awareness of bereavement. The vastness of the suffering of humankind is staggering to the mind even to think about. Thousands die every day from diseases, illnesses, accidents, wars, and deprivation. Even the awareness of the immensity of this problem leads to gloom and depression for many.

Grief can take many forms. In my mind's eye I can still see the young woman as she received the news that her husband had been killed in Vietnam. Alone now with her two small children, they sobbed uncontrollably as they clung to each other. Another form emerges. I see a middle-aged couple whose questions in the face of their eight-year-old daughter's death from leukemia are not so easily or quickly answered. "Why? We waited so long for a child and she was the only one we could have. Why? It doesn't make any sense." From a hospital bed comes the voice of another that I remember. "I cannot understand what I must have done to be punished, to suffer like this." The eyes of another young lady expressed the grief she was experiencing as she told of admitting her husband to the psychiatric ward of a hospital because of a nervous break- down. Another sat across the desk and could not hold back the tears as she wept over her marriage and the infidelity and brutality of her husband.

Unfortunately the list could go on because suffering, pain, sin, death, and grief are a part of life that none of us escapes. They march across the line of our vision and sooner or later into the lives of us all. Grief sometimes bursts into our lives through a terrible catastrophe such as an automobile accident, or we can sense it gradually ap- proaching in the failing health of loved ones. Grief may slam doors we had planned to enter, shatter dreams we had clung to, destroy carefully laid plans, darken the brightest of days, and hurl us into a world which seems to have formed a conspiracy of silence toward us and our aches.

A Strange Beatitude

The words of this Beatitude, "Blessed are they that mourn: for they shall be comforted" (KJV), seem astonish- ing. How can one speak of the happiness of grief, the joy of sorrow, or the delight of sadness? This startling Beati- tude seems to run counter not only to the modern world's vision of happiness but appears to be at odds even with common sense. What kind of sorrow brings happiness? What sort of pain brings glee? Is this passage the proof text for those who seem to enjoy poor health and delight in their misery? But this morbid attitude really focuses more on the desire for self-pity than happiness. Is this passage the touch pole of the sad-faced Christians who see no joy, radiance, or gaiety in the Christian faith? Are we to equate sad eyes, long faces, heavy spirits, dull dress, a grave stance, dejected attitude, and melancholy conversation with the Christian life? Although some have approached the Christian faith from this perspective, it seems difficult to reconcile this with the words where Jesus said, "These things have I spoken unto you, that my joy might remain in you, and that your joy might be full" (John 15:11, KJV).

The kingdom of God reverses and challenges our thinking about life. This Beatitude probes us to do more than readjust our appearance and dress. It turns our values upside down and opens our nerve ends to personal sorrow and to the suffering of humanity. It introduces us to an inner joy and peace which is realized only after our grief has been transformed. The joy and happiness which Jesus promises comes about not by fleeing from pain and grief, but in experiencing the depths of sorrow and loss and then knowing the joy and consolation of divine love.

The loss of a loved one in and of itself is difficult, not joyful or happy. The blessedness the mourner experiences comes about when out of his feelings of discord the counterbalance of a new peace and happiness is finally attained. "In life, as in music," Theodore H. Robinson observed, "the most perfect form of peace is that which is brought by the resolved discord. For the comfort of God is not the use of conventional formulas of consolation; it is the perfect sympathy of one who has sounded the uttermost depths of pain."[1] In grief, however, a person comes to realize that he or she has gained a new experience which could be known only through sorrow. And one also is aware that the experience of consolation could not be known apart from his or her own personal acquaintance with grief. It is a kind of joy which is not known except through the tragedy of personal experience. No one else can stand in for us or shoulder totally the load for us.

Grief is always personal but so is the comfort which Jesus promised in this second Beatitude. Even in the sunlight the stars are still shining but they are not visible to our eyes. The darkness of the night, however, soon exposes them to us. Sometimes there are experiences which remain unknown to us in the brilliant sunlight of ordinary living. When the dark night of grief overshadows us, then the starry presence of another dimension is revealed to us—maybe for the first time, and always in a deeper way.

Sorrow For Sin

Grief does take many forms. One of the meanings of this Beatitude might be expressed in these words: "Blessed are they who mourn for their sins for they shall be comforted." Since the Beatitude follows the blessings of God on the poor in spirit, sorrow for one's sin could be a key emphasis that Jesus was stressing. When we are moved to sorrow by the realization of our sins, then the comfort of forgiveness is near. Many today, however, feel no sense of regret or remorse, no guilt or disgrace, no thought of dishonor or humiliation, no shame or reproach, and remain insensitive to wrong or offense.

They are like a man who was isolated in the frozen Northwest. He knew he was all right as long as feeling remained in his feet as he struggled forward in the deep snows while the bitter freezing weather beat down upon him. When the pain finally left his feet, he knew, however, that it was too late to help them. As they slowly froze, the pain lessened. His pain, ache, and hurt were signs of life. When he reached the point that they were past feeling, he realized how desperate his situation was.

This is one of society's difficulties today. We have become insensitive to sin. Dr. Karl Menninger, the renowned psychistrist of the Menninger Clinic, has attempted to awaken modern persons to the immense damage which has been done by our attempt to avoid, ignore, disguise, and hide from the awful reality of sin.

The Christian faith has taught through the centuries the reality of sin and its corruption. But in recent years many have chosen to place the blame for man and woman's immoral behavior and corrupt nature at the doorstep of illness, illegality, heredity, genes, environment, society, subconsciousness, unconsciousness, irresponsibility, or the like. The word *sin* has been carefully and deliberately avoided. Dr. Menninger has addressed himself to this very problem in his extraordinary book, *Whatever Became of Sin?* The recognition of the reality of sin, according to Menninger, would enable society to treat both the mental and moral health of persons. His call is for a renewed understanding of the nature of the reality of sin both on a personal and social level.

T. S. Eliot, in his play *The Cocktail Party,* told of a young woman, Celia, who engaged in conversation with a psychiatrist, named Reilly, whom she had met at the cocktail party. Celia acknowledged that many of her motives had been wrong but because she lived in a community where sin had disappeared from society's vocabulary, she had difficulty in locating the cause of her actions. Finally, she concluded that her problem might be sin. When pressed, though, Celia was unable to tell what she meant by *sin.* Nothing in her background had prepared her to find the wellspring of wrong motives in sin. Instead, she had learned to believe that anything wrong was bad form or caused by something psychological. As she talked, Celia at last came closer to the root of her problem. She observed that she felt a certain emptiness, a sense of failure toward someone or something outside of herself.[2] The New Testament calls that "someone" or "something" *God.*

"Have the men of our time still a feeling of the meaning of sin?" asked the theologian Paul Tillich. "Do we still realize that sin does *not* mean an immoral act, that 'sin' should never be used in the plural, and that not our sins, but rather our *sin* is the great, all-pervading problem of our life?"[3] Tillich continued by defining sin as "separation" in a threefold sense: separation from others, separation of a person from one's self, and separation from God. Nevertheless, there are sins, and sin cannot exist in the abstract. There is sin only where there are sinners and sinning such as greed, lust, hate, envy, prejudice, and so forth. Those who mourn are aware of their separated nature and have found the wholeness that bridges the gap between one's own self, others, and God.

In Alan Paton's beautifully moving novel, *Cry, the Beloved Country,* the black African minister Stephen Kumalo has just visited his son who has been imprisoned because of murder. An anguished cry rises from Kumalo's lips as he speaks with a fellow minister.

> He is a stranger. . . . I cannot touch him, I cannot reach him. I see no shame in him, no pity for those he has hurt. Tears come out of his eyes, but it seems that he weeps only for himself, not for his wickedness, but for his danger.
>
> The man cried out, can a person lose all sense of evil? A boy, brought up as he was brought up? I see only his pity for himself, he who has made two children fatherless.[4]

What has happened to our sense of evil? "The greatest security against sin," Thomas Carlyle once remarked, "is to be shocked at its presence." Few are shocked anymore. The question is no longer whether something is moral or immoral; we attempt to locate ourselves in the center and assume that all acts are merely amoral. Good and evil are not seen in colors of black and white, but everything is depicted now in shades of gray. We feel we are too mature today to talk of sin, so we speak of wrongs which are done as being merely the result of errors, mistakes, sickness, heredity, environment, or the like.

Is no one any longer responsible for his or her own acts of wrongdoing? Menninger has challenged B. F. Skinner's contention that there is no personal decision involved in behavior and consequently no guilt or responsibility. As an analogy he asked,

> If a dozen people are in a lifeboat and one of them discovers a leak near where he is sitting, is there any doubt as to his responsibility? Not for having *made* the hole, or for finding it, but for attempting to repair it! To ignore it or to keep silent about it is almost equivalent to having made it![5]

Identifying some act as sin does have value, according to Menninger because "it identifies something to be eliminated or avoided." It also acknowledges that it is not just the criminals or neurotics who need to be dealt with but that everyone has the responsibility of answering for the rightness or wrongness of his or her own actions. "Yes, a conscious sense of guilt, and implicit or explicit repentance," Menninger declared, "would be consequences of the revival of an acknowledgement of error, transgression, offense and responsibility—in short, of sin. This is the answer to the reader's question—'So what?' This is one difference it would make."[6]

When the first atomic bomb was exploded in the desert near Los Alamos, Dr. Robert Oppenheimer said that he recalled a passage from the *Bhagavad Gita*, "I am become death, the shatterer of worlds." The aftermath of this experience left him with a "legacy of concern." "In some sort of crude sense which no vulgarity, no humor, no overstatement can quite extinguish," he asserted, "the physicists have known sin: and this is a knowledge which they cannot lose."[7] Here is witnessed a sense of responsibility which affirms the awesome reality of evil.

I think Tillich was correct: "There is a mysterious fact about the great words of our religious tradition: they cannot be replaced. All attempts to make substitutions including those I have tried myself have failed to convey the reality that was to be expressed; they have led to shallow and impotent talk. There are no substitutes for words like sin and grace."[8]

Most of us live with the illusion that we can easily overcome any habit we may have, throw off quickly all negative characteristics, break loose without difficulty from our misdeeds. But such is rarely the case. Charles Schulz depicted our modern difficulty with freeing self from sin in a conversation between Linus and Lucy. Lucy speaks with Linus who is standing near her holding his blanket and sucking his thumb. "Linus, there's still time for you to make a New Year's resolution to give up that blanket." "You know I think you're right!" Linus says, "I think if I'm ever going to get rid of it *now* is the time! So I'll just *throw* it away and be done with it once and for all!" So he tosses it to the side, but a long string is attached to one corner of the blanket and to his hand. For a moment he stands smiling until he slowly begins to perspire and become very nervous. Then he turns and quickly begins pulling the blanket toward himself. Standing again with blanket in hand and thumb in his mouth, Linus declares, "Never believe anything I say!"[9]

It is never easy to throw off our sins. We notice that we slip back constantly into old habits, follow blind trails, frequent bad companions, reach back for what we once thought were forgotten means, assent to words that we said we would never agree with. Sin has a hold on us that is stronger than we can ever explain. Paul spoke of the dilemma of every person when he declared: "For I know that nothing good dwells within me, that is, in my flesh. I can will what is right, but I cannot do it. For I do not do the good I want, but the evil I do not want is what I do. Now if I do what I do not want, it is no longer I that do it, but sin which dwells within me" (Rom. 7:18-20).

I can still see the faces of several young people as I have talked to them about their problems with drugs. "I don't want to offend you, Pastor," one of them said, "but I can control this thing. You just have some naive ideas about drugs." Later I walked with this lad's family, and others, along pathways of personal agony which were carved by this kind of attitude. Our habits, mannerisms, weaknesses, and sins become a part of us which we cannot ignore nor deny. "I won't count this time!" someone may say to himself after yielding to temptation. "He may not count it, and a kind Heaven may not count it," the psychologist William James once observed, "but it is being counted nonetheless. Down among his nerve-cells and fibers the molecules are counting it, registering, storing it up to be used against him when the next temptation comes."[10]

Years ago in a wilderness section of Canada a sign was posted along a dirt road: "Choose your rut, you'll be in it for the next twenty miles." This advice is true also for the habits of daily life. Choose carefully your habit pathways because soon the pathway becomes a track and then a roadway, then an avenue, then an expressway, and eventually a rut. Our thoughts and actions, our dreams and activities, our work and leisure are molding our character every moment of every day. We are slowly building the nature of our character one step at a time. "Habit," Augustine observed, "if not resisted, soon becomes necessity."[11]

We must choose wisely the rut to which we want to commit our lives so that it will be a pathway of progress and meaning and not a channel which leads to the destruction and death of our authentic personhood. "Habit is a cable," Horace Mann once observed. "We weave a thread of it every day, and at last we cannot break it."

A life dominated only by uncontrolled desires is an unhappy and discordant one. Real happiness is possible when the direction and drives of our inner selves are guided by the higher way of Jesus. For many of us it is not easy to admit that we have done anything wrong or need any help outside our own resources. Isn't this the problem Schulz raised when he had Peppermint Patty say, "Ray, I need some good advice. What do you do when something you've counted on doesn't happen? This thing I really believed was going to happen, didn't happen. What do I do?" "Well," says Ray, "you could admit you were wrong." "Besides that, I mean," says Peppermint Patty. Clinging to our illusions, establishing our defenses, marshaling our denials, or fortifying our excuses seems to be our common approach rather than admitting that we have made a mistake, failed, or sinned.

An observer one freezing winter day noticed a bird of prey light on a floating carcass in the Niagara River below Buffalo. As the bird fed on the carcass it was aware of the great falls near at hand, but it intended to fly away before it reached the dangerous point. When the thunder of the falls was near, the giant bird stretched its wings to fly away from the imminent danger. But it was too late. The bird's talons had frozen to the carcass it had been feeding on. He was swept over the rapids with the creature to which he was attached.

This describes the familiar problem of our destruction by habits which we believed we could control or keep in bay. "Sow an act," George Dana Boardman once noted, "and you reap a habit; sow a habit, and you reap a character; sow a character, and you reap a destiny."

Those who mourn for their sins are aware of the pain

they have caused themselves, others, and God. With a sense of a broken heart they ask for forgiveness. Sensitive to our own needs, we can then say with the psalmist: "For I will declare mine iniquity; I will be sorry for my sin" (Ps. 38:18, KJV). And another, "My sin is ever before me" (Ps. 51:3). The apostle Paul declared the mourner's awareness of "salvation" (2 Cor. 7:10). Paul voiced every person's cry when he declared: "Who will deliver me from this body of death?" His answer came quickly. "The law of the Spirit of life in Christ Jesus has set me free from the law of sin and of death" (Rom. 7:24; 8:2). In acknowledgement of our sins, we echo the publican's words: "God be merciful to me a sinner!" (Luke 18:13).

One of the benefits of the old mourner's bench was the fact that it served as a place where one could confess his or her sins to God and experience pardon. Benjamin Garrison set forth a rather strong argument in favor of some concrete method of expressing forgiveness to one who has confessed his or her sins. "The certainty of restoration," he avowed, "is an indispensable part of forgiveness." To illustrate his point he told about a young woman who came to him tortured with the guilt of her illegitimate child whose birth she had kept a secret even from the father. Dr. Garrison indicated that he listened long and spoke of the forgiving love of God but to no avail. "Finally," he said, "moved by an unmistakable prompting, I took her to the chapel and knelt with her in prayer. Then I stood while she still knelt, placed my hand upon her head and said, 'Rebecca,' (this was, of course, not her name) 'Rebecca, I forgive you in the name of God. Now go, and live as a forgiven woman.' "12

This reminds us of the words of Jesus to the woman caught in the act of adultery. "Neither do I condemn you; go, and do not sin again" (John 8:11). Sometimes a visible act of restoration, whether it is the spoken words of a minister to one plagued with guilt, a public stand in a church service by one who has sinned, a response to an altar call, or the verbal acceptance by a church congregation of a penitent one, may be the triggering factor in enabling a sinner to experience forgiveness.

Today many feel too sophisticated and modern to talk about sin. A college girl reacted to a lecture by a visiting minister on her campus by explaining to a friend: "What in the world was the preacher talking about when he said we are sinners? What is sin?" Many today want a "no-fault" morality life-style. Within us and within our world exist problems and enigmas of all kinds, and we had rather ignore them or assume no responsibility for them. Though we may avoid the word, can we so easily escape the awareness of our own sin and need for forgiveness? The sins of the flesh like murder, theft, rape, and adultery are visible acts. But our real problem with sin may lie more in the area of temperament. My struggle and your struggle might be concerned more with sins related to disposition and attitudes, jealousies and hatreds, or vindictiveness and pettiness.

Our social sins cannot be overlooked—the problems of war, pollution, crime, poverty, slums, racism, and others. "There is no telling to what extremes of cruelty and ruthlessness a man will go," observed Eric Hoffer, "when he is freed from the fears, hesitations, doubts and the vague stirrings of decency that go with individual judgment. When we lose our individual independence in the corporateness of a mass movement, we find a new freedom— freedom to hate, bully, lie, torture, murder and betray without shame or remorse."[13]

There are also the sins of neglect. Think of the sins of things we should have done but neglected to do, such as people to whom we should give a helping hand, words we should have said, letters we should have written, the handshake we should have extended, the help to someone we knew had a pain, sorrow, or burden.

No one is able to mourn for his sin until he is aware that he has a need. When each of us has rediscovered his or her own sense of sin and honestly faced one's own need, then spiritual healing can begin. Jesus indicated that His blessing of comfort is to be given to those who take sin seriously. To mourn for sin is to feel, to care, and deplore the awful disorder it has inflicted upon us. It is to acknowledge that we are the problem—with our selfishness, prejudice, hatred, shame, perversions, hostility, violence, and buried resentments. It is to declare with the swamp character Pogo, "We have met the enemy and he is us." It is to join with Isaiah and confess, "All we like sheep have gone astray; we have turned every one to his own way" (Is. 53:6). It is to affirm the poverty of spirit which we have and confess our absolute dependence upon God.

Forgiveness can only follow a heart that expresses sorrow for its sin. When a person comes to God in the sorrow of repentance for one's sins, he or she receives the comfort of God's forgiving love and is filled with the presence of God to face future temptations. The English word *comfort* comes from two Latin words *con fortis* which mean "with strength." The comfort which Christ gives us fortifies us with the strength of His presence. The apostle Paul understood this comfort when he said, "I can do all things in him who strengthens me" (Phil 4:13).

The Tears of Grief

Most of us have sat by the bedside of a parent, a child, a wife or husband, a friend—someone we have loved, who is now gone—and experienced the agony of grief. Grief is no illusion; it is very real. No one who lives can finally escape it. It visits the home of every person. The dark night of sorrow touches every home sooner or later. Everyone searches for what Joshua Liebman has described as "the slow wisdom of grief."[14]

Our busy modern world does not allow us much time for grief, and it tries to force us to handle our bereavement quickly. This, of course, is difficult to do. So instead of meeting and dealing with it, many suppress their grief feelings deep within themselves. The shock of grief pulls a person in different directions, and one is not certain which way to turn. We may have conflicting feelings of calm and shock, confidence and depression, faith and doubt, trust and anxiety, peace and anger, memories and dreams, hopes and cares, and many others. These paradoxical feelings are normal and need not make us feel guilty. As a normal person, we will grieve, but as a Christian we affirm: "Sorrow not even as others which have no hope" (1 Thess. 4:13, KJV).

He found the words difficult to say as I put my arm around his shoulder: "She's dead. I can't believe it." His wife had been dying for months with cancer and only a few moments after Mr. Jones arrived again at the hospital his wife took her last breath. It had been a long, difficult experience for the whole family. Now she was dead. The words did not come easily. "The children must know. What do I do now?" he asked me. What he did was to face his loss and reach within for the spiritual resources which had given him strength in other crises. Now he had to begin the slow, painful journey of working through his sorrow.

She is dead. The words are difficult to learn and even more difficult to say. A young college student said to me recently, "People act so strangely toward me when I tell them that my mother is dead. If I say she has 'passed away' or has 'expired' they do not seem so shocked, but they recoil at the words, 'she's dead.' " Even as Christians we must admit the reality of death. This is not to say that we welcome it or can fully explain it. But it is an acknowledgement that death is a part of life.

To conquer our grief, we must first be willing to acknowledge and face it. Camouflaging or disguising it will not make it disappear. Whether it is the starving child across the ocean, or a stranger across town, a neighbor down the street, a friend next door, or one of our relatives, grief comes to us all. "What man shall live," asked the psalmist, "and not see death?" (Ps. 89:48, NEB)? We can identify with the prophet Jeremiah and declare, "This is [my grief] and I must bear it" (Jer. 10:19).

Birds like the cardinal, blue jay, chickadee, and others are able to survive the cold of winter because they know to turn their faces into the wind. If they turned their backs to the freezing winter winds, snow, and freezing rain would penetrate their feathers and get next to the body and soon freeze the birds. By facing the storm, the feathers are matted tightly together and this holds the warmth of the body in and wards off the fierce winds. None of the problems of life, grief included, are met by turning away from them, or by ignoring them, or by refusing to acknowledge that they exist. Instead of facing one's sorrow, some turn to alcohol, drugs, sexual adventures, or other unsatisfying solutions. Spiritual health can begin when we have taken the first step by acknowledging the reality of death and the reality of our own grief.

Often, when someone has experienced grief, advice is given to them such as "put it out of your mind," "don't think about it," or "try to forget it." Not only can we not do that, but we should not. Healing comes more quickly when we do not try to forget our loss or deny our ache but begin instead the process of facing our memories by slowly doing whatever is necessary to process what the deceased owned, visiting familiar places once shared, looking at family pictures, focusing on favorite possessions, and other sometimes painful procedures. To forget the loss means also forgetting the joys, the happiness, the loves which one once experienced.

A story from ancient Greek mythology taught this lesson centuries ago. At her death a woman appeared before Charon, the ferryman, who was to carry her across the Styx River. Charon informed her that she could now drink from the waters of Lethe which would enable her to forget all that she had ever known. "Ah," she said, "then I can forget how much I have suffered." "Yes," he replied, "and you will also forget how much you have rejoiced." "Ah," she said, "but I can forget all my failures." "Yes," he replied, "and you will also forget your victories." "Ah," she said, "but I can forget how often I have been hated." "Yes," he replied, "and you will forget how often you have been loved." The woman then decided not to drink from the waters of forgetfulness. Remembering does bring pain for awhile, but it also draws from the recesses of our mind reflections of radiance and joy as well.

In our grief there is also an awareness that we do not suffer alone. Martin Luther translated the Greek word for *mourn* in this Beatitude as *sorrow-bearing,* according to Dietrich Bonhoeffer. "The disciple-community does not shake off sorrow as though it were no concern of its own, but willingly bears it. And in this way they show how close are the bonds which bind them to the rest of humanity."[15] In the church, the community of faith, there is concern and support for all who suffer or mourn. We lean upon each other and seek to help one another bear the sorrows that all of us sooner or later must face.

Albert Schweitzer, the medical missionary to the African jungle, once expressed his feelings of the church's responsibility for bearing the burdens and pains of humanity. "I could not but feel with a sympathy full of regret all the pain that I saw around me," Schweitzer wrote, "not only that of men but that of the whole creation. From this community of suffering I have never tried to withdraw myself. It has seemed to me a matter of course, that we should all take our share of the burden of pain which lies upon the world."[16]

On many occasions I have seen the shadow of grief fall across the pathway of church members only to see others move in with the sunshine of their presence to bear them up during this ordeal. I remember a young couple who had lost their son in an accident, who later went to help another couple who were passing though the dark night of a similar experience. On many occasions I have seen a widow go to the home of a friend to share with her the inner strength which she found in her encounter with grief. Mention could be made of many others. We have seen them as they have ministered to others and ourselves.

When grief of any kind enters our life, there is a tendency to withdraw and retreat. But there comes also a time to return to normal activities. This is not easy for the griever either. After Thomas Carlyle had completed writing his masterpiece, *The French Revolution,* he took the manuscript to his neighbor, John Stuart Mill, and asked him to read it. Several days later Mill stood outside Carlyle's door pale and shaken. Mill confessed to his friend that his maid had carelessly used the manuscript to light the morning fire. For days Carlyle was furious as he thought about his two years of work gone up in smoke. The episode had so upset him that he thought that he might never write again. One morning as he was looking out over the skyline of London he noticed a stonemason who was patiently building a wall brick by brick. The sight of this man inspired him to begin anew. He decided that he would not spend his days crying, "This couldn't happen to me!" What had happened had been real, and it was his own experience. His lifelong work had been destroyed, but, like the stonemason, he would begin to rebuild his work bit by bit—page by page. With that spirit he set to work and completed again his monumental study of the French revolution. His experience was one of grief, but he did not let it destroy him. He chose to return to normal living rather than to remain in defeat, remorse, despair, and frustration.

When we experience grief we can allow it to crush us into isolated retreat, or we can rise to walk from our dark valley with a desire to rebuild our lives bit by bit—step by step—day by day. In the midst of the tears of our grief, we recognize death as a part of life and seek to affirm with Job; "The Lord gave, and the Lord has taken away; blessed be the name of the Lord" (Job 1:21).

There are no easy answers to the problem of evil, pain, suffering, grief, and death. The basic issue in grief is never a rational probe anyway. Questions race to our minds demanding answers which seldom come. Suggestions are offered by friends or relatives which leave huge gaps in our search for reasonable solutions to illogical enigmas. "Whys" surface in our minds if they do not reach our lips. We want to know "why," but wonder if we should. And we often feel guilty when the doubts flash through our mind.

When L. D. Johnson received the crushing news of the death of his twenty-three-year-old daughter, Carole, in an icy highway accident, he waited sixteen years before he wrote about his own struggles with that tragic loss. He offered no easy answers. "The mystery of unmerited suffering remains; I know of no satisfactory explanation." He found the "answer" in the incarnation, death, and resurrection of Jesus Christ.

God in Christ took our sin and suffering upon himself.

He has not abolished the hurts of human existence, but he has shared them and identified himself with our plight. He did not change the order of the universe to make evil impossible and thus destroy man's humanity by taking away his freedom. Instead he partook of the cup of suffering himself and gave us the promise that nothing in all creation can separate us from his love.[17]

The Comfort of God

"Blessed are they that mourn; for they shall be comforted" (KJV). When grief comes to us it is uniquely our own, but the Christian is aware that he or she does not have to face sorrow alone. We have the assurance of the presence of another—God Himself. The Christian is not offered an insurance plan against all difficulties, or a safety area which will guard him or her from all illness and sorrow, or an inoculation program to protect each of us from all bumps and bruises. What Christ does offer to us is His own presence. In the darkness of grief, sometimes it is not always easy to have absolute certainty of God's presence. But Jesus has assured us that He is the Good Shepherd and that He will help shoulder our burden and sorrow. Jesus has directed us to cast our burdens on Him and He will sustain us (Matt. 11:28-30).

When I was in college, I had the opportunity one Sunday to preach in a small, rural, mountain church in Virginia. As I began the climb up the steep mountain, I met patches of fog that became a heavy cover within a few miles. The further I went, the worse the fog got. Several times I had to stop my car and get out to make certain I was still on the road. I moved cautiously up the mountainous road through the fog until a small flicker of light began to break through the fog. Suddenly as I reached the top of the mountain the fog disappeared and sunshine filled my car with all of its brilliance and drove away the fog around me and within me. At that moment an insight dawned that has lingered since that day. The sun is always shining. Even when the fog blocks out the sun and hides its radiance, it should not cause one to question its existence. It continues to shine behind the blanket of fog.

For me this became a parable about the presence of God. If the darkness of grief overshadows us, or the fog of sorrowful depression overtakes us, God is still there, just as the sun continues to shine above the fog. We should never forget that great truth. God is still with us in the midst of our sorrow to comfort and sustain us. In the words from Isaiah, we sing of Jesus in Handel's *Messiah* as "a man of sorrows and acquainted with grief." His spirit is sensitive to our need.

It is a shame that we have forgotten the original meaning for the word *comfort* and have softened it to mean comfortable. Those who experience the comfort of Christ find a peace that comes from strength because they have been fortified by the power of His presence. Jesus indeed is the one who is able to "comfort my people" (Isa. 40:1). The promises of our Lord give us assurance in the midst of our sorrow.

> So you have sorrow now, but I will see you again and your hearts will rejoice, and no one will take your joy from you (John 16:22).

> Peace I leave with you; my peace I give to you; not as the world gives do I give to you. Let not your hearts be troubled, neither let them be afraid (John 14:27).

In the Gospel of Matthew Jesus issued an appeal for all to come to Him for the strength and support His presence can give to us when our load is heavy.

> Come to me, all whose work is hard, whose load is heavy; and I will give you relief. Bend your necks to my yoke, and

learn from me, for I am gentle and humble-hearted; and your souls will find relief. For my yoke is good to bear, my load is light (Matt. 11:28-30, NEB).

Some Greek scholars have translated part of this passage to read "my yoke is well adjusted." In ancient Palestine and even in some sections of the Eastern world today, farmers have often used what is known as a "training yoke." When a younger, inexperienced animal, such as an ox, was being trained for a farming animal, the training yoke was so designed that the heavier load was placed on the shoulders of the stronger and more experienced animal and the younger bore the lighter load. As long as he kept parallel with the other animal and did not attempt to wander out of the furrow where they were plowing, the yoke would be easy for him and would not chafe the younger animal's shoulders. The yoke was "good to bear," or "well adjusted" as long as the younger animal was willing to allow the older, wiser, and stronger animal to lead.

Often grief and suffering become a load which is too heavy to bear because we attempt to carry the whole load by ourselves. None of us has ever used all of his strength until he has utilized the power that comes from the presence of God in his life. "Blessed are they that mourn; for they shall be comforted" (KJV). The comfort which God gives to us provides an inner strength. It enables us to face any situation because we are assured that we do not have to meet it isolated or alone. "Who shall separate us from the love of Christ?" cried Paul.

Shall tribulation, or distress, or persecution, or famine, or nakedness, or peril, or sword? No, in all these things we are more than conquerors through him who loved us. For I am sure that neither death, nor life, nor angels, nor principalities, nor things present, nor things to come, nor powers, nor heights, nor depth, nor anything else in all creation, will be able to separate us from the love of God in Christ Jesus our Lord (Rom. 8:35, 37-39).

To expect to find joy in grief seems astonishing. However, the Christian becomes aware in the midst of his or her sorrow of an inner consolation which is unknown outside the experience of a comforted griever. Those who mourn for their sins are those who are able to experience the comfort of forgiveness and pardon because they have honestly confessed their dependence upon God. Every life has met grief in some form or other. The Christian does not have to carry his or her load by one's self but each of us has the assurance of the presence of God to strengthen and undergird us in the midst of one's grief and tragedy. Under the yoke of Christ we know that we are to live with a sense of inner peace. "Cast your burden on the Lord, and he will sustain you" (Ps. 55:22).

Notes

1. Theodore H. Robinson, *The Gospel of Matthew* (New York: Harper and Brothers, 1927), p. 29.

2. T. S. Eliot, *The Cocktail Party* (New York: Harcourt, Brace and Company, 1950), pp. 134-137.

3. Paul Tillich, *The Shaking of the Foundations* (New York: Charles Scribner's Sons, 1948), p. 154.

4. Alan Paton, *Cry, the Beloved Country* (New York: Charles Scribner's Sons, 1948), p. 109.

5. Karl Menninger, *Whatever Became of Sin?* (New York: Hawthorn Books, Inc., 1973), p. 179.

6. *Ibid., p. 187.*

7. *Time,* November 8, 1948.

8. Tillich, *op. cit.,* pp. 153-154.

9. Charles Schulz, *Peanuts,* United Feature Syndicate, Inc., 1966.

10. *The Philosophy of William James,* "Education and Behavior," (New York: The Modern Library, 1953), pp. 285-2;86.

11. *Saint Augustine's Confessions.* book 8, ch. 5 (10). translated by Vernon J. Bourke. (N.Y.: Fathers of the Church, Inc.) p. 206.

12. R. Benjamin Garrison, *Worldly Holiness* (Nashville: Abingdon Press, 1972), pp. 46-47.

13. Eric Hoffer, *The True Believer*, (New York: Mentor Books, 1951), p. 93.

14. Joshua Liebman, *Peace of Mind* (New York: Simon and Schuster, 1946) pp. 105ff.

15. Dietrich Bonhoeffer, *The Cost of Discipleship* (London: SCM Press, Ltd, 1959), p. 98.

16. Albert Schweitzer, *Out of My Life and Thought* (New York: Mentor Book, 1949), p. 186.

17. L. D. Johnson, *The Morning After Death* (Nashville: Broadman Press, 1978), p. 113.

Lord, I feel that my life is so drab and colorless, lived so far from a time when there were wars of faith and deeds of heroism. Help me to see with truth what cosmic battles are being waged in my own day and in the very environment where I live. Then let me make my commitment to follow Christ and fulfill it every hour, that I may not lose my soul in the mindless routine of days. For his name's sake. Amen.

John Killinger, *His Power in You.*

3

Disciplined Strength

Blessed are the meek, for they shall inherit the earth (Matt. 5:5).

"I'm going to make my mark in the world," the young student said to me. Then taking a stick, he scratched a deep furrow in the ground. "My place in this world will be as visible as that. I'll make money and have status and power. People will say, 'There goes an important guy. He is somebody.' "

Like this young man, many of us today judge success in terms of power and strength. We seem to have come into the world with our fists clenched and stand ready to fight for our rights. We are going to be number one even if we have to walk all over other people's rights or privileges. In the face of militant nations, worldwide communism, the rise of crime, business aggressiveness, and the competitive nature of modern persons, meekness appears foolish and maybe even cowardly. The blessedness of the meek, however, may be the most misunderstood Beatitude.

Meekness Is Not Weakness

A small boy turned to his mother, who insisted on calling him "my little lamb," and exclaimed: "Mother, I don't want to be your little lamb. I want to be your little tiger." Meekness is generally seen as softness or weakness. Our colloquialisms reveal our understanding of the word

65

meekness. The phrase, "He is as meek as a mouse," depicts an unattractive frightened creature that lives in the darkness and shadows and survives off the leftovers of others. When someone says that you are as "meek as a lamb," that remark is seldom taken as a compliment. Lambs may be thought of as soft, sweet, and lovable animals, but they are noted also for their helpless nature. Casper Milquetoast, of comic-strip fame, epitomized the popular image of meekness to the modern mind. Here was a pathetic figure who was taken advantage of by everyone, whether he was at work, on the street, or at home. He literally trembled at the sound of the voice of his bullying wife. This is the idea that most people have of meekness.

Schulz's Charlie Brown is the contemporary version of the Milquetoast mentality. In a recent cartoon Charlie Brown stood before his class in school giving a report. "My subject today is glaciers," he said. "Glaciers are huge rivers of ice. A glacier will frequently move forward one foot while retreating three feet . . . which reminds me a lot of myself."[1] A meek person is seen as one who can be pushed around, walked over, abused, sneered at, insulted, and mishandled without anticipating any response from him. No one admires this kind of person. He is usually pitied or laughed at.

David H. C. Read stated that a woman once remarked to him in a Scottish church that a certain young man was going to enter the ministry. "I'm so pleased," the woman said to Dr. Read, "he's just the type—a nice, harmless boy he always was."[2] Can it be possible that Jesus is saying that those who are weak, spineless, submissive, and cowardly are the blessed who will inherit the earth? How absurd this Beatitude must sound, then, to modern persons. However, if this is our understanding of it, maybe we had better raise the question of whether or not we have heard the original tone correctly. The biblical meaning of meekness needs to be understood before this Beatitude is so quickly judged and more easily rejected.

Jesus lifted the word *meekness*, according to A. T. Robertson, the Greek scholar, "to a nobility never attained before."[3] "And which has been lost again to modern society" are words that need to be added to Robertson's sentence. Meekness in the biblical sense was never equated with weakness but with strength. Jesus referred to Himself as "meek and lowly in heart" (Matt. 11:29, KJV), and Moses was also called the meekest of men (Num. 12:3). Their meekness was not in any way associated with timidity, effeminacy, subservience, lack of courage, fragility, or weakness but was seen as strength united with gentleness. Both stood fearless in the face of opposition and in humble trust were committed to the will of God for their lives.

Moses defied the throne of Pharaoh in Egypt, and Jesus refused to surrender to the power of Rome or Jerusalem. Who would dare call them spineless, weak, timid, or harmless? Meek, yes. Weak, no! The meek, Frank Stagg stated, "are those who under the pressures of life have learned to bend their wills and to set aside their own notions as they stand before the greatness and grace of God."[4] Moses and Jesus are two great biblical figures who had learned to do this and can be correctly called meek men. "Meekness cannot well be counterfeited," said William Swan Plumer. "It is not insensibility, or unmanliness, or servility: it does not cringe, or whine. It is benevolence imitating Christ in patience, forbearance, and quietness."

Submission to God

Pride is man and woman's basic sin. It is what keeps us from following God and seeking His guidance of our lives. We are constantly asserting arrogantly our desire to be independent of God and go it alone. How naive is our notion of independence! Everyone of us is dependent upon many others for most of the essentials and luxuries which we have. Our dependency is clearly evident in our reliance upon the farmer, grocer, manufacturer, merchant, clerk, postman, banker, carpenter, mechanic, teacher, and many thousands of other nameless persons. "The beautiful must ever rest in the arms of the sublime," Harriet Beecher Stowe once observed. "The gentle need the strong to sustain it, as much as the rock-flowers need rocks to grow on, or the ivy the rugged wall which it embraces."

We often say that someone is of independent means. None of us really is. We are all dependent upon others for so much of what we have, where we go, the means by which we travel, the education we receive, the clothes we wear, the food we eat, the books we read, the music we listen to, or even the recreation we pursue. In our world neighborhood we share in the labors of others. Absolute independence in our modern, mechanized society is an illusion which is quickly shattered when something breaks down or is out of stock, sold out, beyond repair, won't fit, or is too big, too small, misplaced, stolen, lost, or simply won't work, run, stop, start, or stand. "There is, in short, no dimension of existence in which the individual is purely an individual," Reinhold Niebuhr said, "and is not in need of either material or spiritual and moral support from some community."[5]

In a larger sense, we are all aware that we cannot live without submitting to the natural laws God has created within His universe. Whether you like it or not, the law of gravity will work if you fall off the roof while repairing it, and you may break an arm or a leg. Several years ago, when my daughter was eight years old, she fell out of a tree and landed on her arm and broke it. She looked up at me and said, "Daddy, I wish this was a dream." But it was not. When we fall and land the wrong way, occasionally something will be broken.

None of us can live independently of the natural laws. A farmer who expects to reap a harvest must learn to plant his crops in cooperation with the seasons and not in defiance of them. This is a form of meekness. To try to plant a garden during the wrong season of the year is not freedom or independence but ignorance and waste.

God has established not only natural but moral and spiritual laws within which we must learn to live and function. To do otherwise is to invite self-destruction. We are all such self-willed persons that it is difficult to admit our need for strength beyond our own resources. Few of us are willing to admit our mistakes, failures, sins, or poor judgments. In another one of Charles Schulz's comic strips on "Peanuts," Lucy and Charlie Brown are walking along talking. In his conversation Charlie Brown says, "I hate having so many faults . . . I'd really like to be a better person. I wonder what it would be like to know that you were perfect." With a smirk on her face, Lucy responds, "Take it from me, it's a great feeling."[6]

Maybe most of us are not that arrogant about ourselves to others, but we do have the same basic problem of pride. The meekness Jesus is describing in this Beatitude is submission to God's will and laws. It is the poverty of spirit which acknowledges our dependence upon God for everything we have and are.

"We must not think Pride is something God forbids because He is offended at it, or that Humility is something He demands as due to His own dignity—as if God Himself was proud," declared C. S. Lewis. "He is not in the least worried about His dignity. The point is, He wants you to know Him; wants to give you Himself."[7] Lewis continued by giving a revised image of a "humble" person.

Do not imagine that if you meet a really humble man he will be what most people call "humble" nowadays; he will not be a sort of greasy, smarmy person, who is always telling you that, of course, he is nobody. Probably all you will think about him is that he seems a cheerful, intelligent chap who took a real interest in what *you* said to *him*. If you do dislike him it will be because you feel a little envious of anyone who seems to enjoy life so easily. He will not be thinking about humility; he will not be thinking about himself at all.

If anyone would like to acquire humility, I can, I think, tell him the first step. The first step is to realize that one is proud. And a biggest step, too. At least, nothing whatever can be done before it. If you think you are not conceited, it means you are very conceited indeed.[8]

Meekness does not describe a cringing soul but one who is aware of his absolute dependence upon God and not himself. John Ruskin expressed this feeling when he said: "All great men not only know their business but usually know that they know it, are not only right in their main contentions but usually know that they are . . . only they do not think much of themselves on that account or expect their fellows to fall down and worship them, for they have a curious undersense of powerlessness, a feeling that the power is not in them but through them."[9]

Most genuinely humble persons do not spend much time thinking about humility but focus instead on what they can do for another and not on what that individual can do for them. They help others to see their own potential and seek to give assistance where there is need, hurt, or pain. Somehow the awareness of their own gifts and greatness does not seem evident in their conversation or deeds. They see a need and have abilities to meet it and reach forward to address that concern without thinking, "how gifted I am to be able to offer help." Their thought is more likely to convey the awareness that they have been merely an instrument which God has found worthy to be used in some helpful way. This is not a view which depreciates their own worth. "True humility is not an object, groveling, self-despising spirit," noted Tryon Edwards. "It is but a right estimate of ourselves as God sees us."[10] The humble person has a high view of another because she has already experienced a noble perception of who she is from God. But the humble person also knows that this dignified view of one's self arises out of a relationship to God. The meek person then, in the sense of this Beatitude, is the first to declare his or her dependence upon God.

Disciplined Strength

The Greek word for *meekness* used by Jesus in this Beatitude does not have an English word which can translate it precisely. This Beatitude can be found originally in Psalm 37:11. Here the Hebrew word for *meek* denotes "being molded." The meek are those who have committed their lives to God and are being molded by Him according to His own purpose for them. The meek person is the humble or lowly individual who freely accepts God's guidance and is thankful for the gifts which God has given him or her. In the New Testament the Greek word for *meek* describes someone or something which has been brought under control. It can be used, for example, to describe a wild horse which has been broken and bridled or a sheep dog which has been trained and domesticated to be obedient to its master. The meek, according to this translation, are those whose wild natures have been brought under the control and training of God.

Martin Luther translated this word into German as "sweet-tempered." The meek is one whose manner and anger are God-controlled. The French use the word, *debonair,* which pictures the Christian gentleman. A gentleman is a *gentle man* who is aware of his strength but has it under control and is not easily provoked.

The manner in which the great Arabian horses are trained indicates powerfully the principle of disciplined strength. After the wild horses are captured from the desert regions and then broken, they are taught to be responsive to certain commands by various signals from a bugle. When the trainer feels satisfied that each animal has learned and responded properly and quickly to the various bugle calls, the horses are placed in a corral overlooking a cool, azure pond. They are kept in the corral, without water, until the drive for thirst is all consuming. Then the gates of the corral are opened, and, as the horses thunder down the slope toward the pool of water, the bugler places the horn to his lips and sounds the call of return. The animals who respond to the signal are then chosen to be among the famous Arabian cavalry brigade.

The meek person, then, is the God-molded, God-trained, God-tempered, and God-disciplined individual. Rather than a weak, cowardly, contemptuous person, Christian meekness denotes one who has great strength but who has his power and strength disciplined under the control of God. Shakespeare had one of his characters express this truth when he observed: "O! it is excellent/To have a giant's strength; but it is tyrannous/To use it like a giant."[11] Christian meekness does not focus primarily on self-control but on God-control. The idea behind this Beatitude is not simply for one to get better control over himself but to allow God to direct and guide himself. Out of the God-controlled life comes greater inner stability, restraint, and self-control.

The meek person has greater control over his or her normal instincts and drives because one is able to draw upon the presence of God within one's life which has brought her or him a new sense of discipline and mastery. The meek person is aware that he or she has power and strength which he or she can use, but it is harnessed and one refuses to use it destructively. This, of course, takes greater courage and control than one who uses his power to push others around like a bull in a china shop.

One of the stories arising out of the Civil War recounts an occasion when President Lincoln went to the home of General McClellan to talk with him about a military matter. General McClellan was away at a reception and Lincoln had to wait for quite awhile. When the general returned, he walked down the hall and, although he had received word that the President was waiting to see him, he went on up the stairs to his bedroom. After waiting for a few more minutes, another message was sent to the general. Word was returned that General McClellan had gone to bed. Lincoln did not speak about McClellan's aloof behavior again. Later when General Lee had defeated the Union Army at the second Battle of Bull Run, and a leader was needed to rebuild the disorganized forces, Lincoln and Halleck went to McClellan and asked him to take charge of the Union Army. Lincoln was asked why he would choose McClellan knowing his attitude of hostility and snobbery toward him. "I will hold McClellan's horse," Lincoln stated, "if he will only bring us success."[12] This is disciplined strength and power under control. Lincoln displayed a spirit of genuine humility. The humble person may have to endure insult or ridicule but his spirit cannot be broken, destroyed, beaten down, or bottled up. He is disciplined to keep on keeping on. Christ does not come into a life to break it but to redirect it.

Jesus was Himself the prime example of one who knew He had unlimited resources but refused to use them for destructive ends. Jesus said, "All power is given unto me in heaven and in earth" (Matt. 28:18, KJV). That is real meekness—disciplined strength. He harnessed His majestic strength and used it in the form of a Servant. With all the resources of heaven at His disposal, He took a towel and basin as His symbol of strength. He came to minister —to serve. His greatest power was seen in His restraint.

Inherit the Earth

"The meek," Jesus said, ". . . shall inherit the earth." If He had said the meek would go to heaven when they died, few would quarrel with that. But His emphasis was clearly that it is the earth which the meek inherit. At first that sounds preposterous. How in the world can the meek inherit the earth? Does the conquest of the earth not belong to the mighty and strong? After Hitler had captured Paris with his armies, he stood overlooking that beautiful city and declared: "Great city! I have conquered her by force; I will now conquer her by love." He was never able to do this. He, along with others who seek to use force to win people, have not yet learned that you cannot compel love or force devotion. God's mastery over our lives has come about by love and grace, not by coercion or defeat.

The kingdom we inherit from Him is received as a gift and is not something we can take by conquest. It is the free gift God gives to all who are His heirs and children. The kingdom we inherit is not some specific territory now or in the future, but is the assurance of life filled with meaning and purpose both in the present and in the future.

When we are arrogant and aggressive, we have not yet found the inner peace and inner strength which comes from the rule of God in our lives. The way of Christ is the avenue of humility, meekness, and service. As the title of Charles Rann Kennedy's play, *The Terrible Meek*, implies, the earth really does belong not to the proud or wealthy but to those who have been willing to follow their Master even when it meant shame, rejection, suffering, or death. The followers of Jesus Christ have what John Milton called "the invincible might of meekness." It is the strength of total commitment to God's will which has now become our own will. "I am come that they might have life, and that they might have it more abundantly" (John 10:10, KJV).

Several years ago there was an old movie on late-night television entitled *Hard Times Texas*. It was about the difficulties of a small Texas town called "Hard Times." Nothing went right in Hard Times. The crops failed, the water dried up, and the people could not get along with each other. One night the town drunk burned down the small town. Everyone, feeling the town was helpless, began to leave. Everyone, that is, but the sheriff. The sheriff went to the edge of town and began stopping the people as they were leaving and saying to them, "I have a great new dream. I'm going to rebuild this town, and I need help." He was able to persuade enough people to join him as he labored to rebuild the town. After the town was rebuilt, the people returned. In this simple story, however, the town drunk also returned and burned down the town again. The story ends with the old sheriff standing by the road stopping the people as they are leaving the city and saying to them, "Hey, I've got a great vision. We're going to rebuild this town."

Jesus Christ offers to us a new dream, a new vision of what life can be like when it is patterned after a way of discipline and love, strength and dependence, humility, and confidence. Although persons might continuously be turning away from the path of life and following the way of destruction, Jesus beckons to us to begin anew. He calls us to keep on keeping on—to fight the forces of evil that right and justice might prevail. The way of Jesus is a challenge to join with God as He is seeking to rebuild the world. He offers to us a vision of what life can really be like when it is modeled after the way of meekness and love instead of coercion and hate.

The Christian life is indeed parodoxical and strange to the minds of many. But we save our lives by surrendering them to Christ, gain by spending them in His cause, receive by giving to others, and live by dying to selfishness. The meek are the inheritors of the earth, because they have received the blessing of a life controlled by God which gives to them discipline, restraint, humility, peace, and confidence.

Notes

1. Charles Schulz, *Peanuts,* United Features Syndicate, Inc., September 18, 1975.

2. David H. C. Read, *The Pattern of Christ* (New York: Charles Scribner's Sons, 1967), p. 27.

3. Archibald Thomas Robertson, *Word Pictures in the New Testament,* Volume I (Nashville: Sunday School Board of the SBC, 1930), p. 41.

4. Frank Stagg, "Matthew," *The Broadman Bible Commentary,* Vol. 8 (Nashville: Broadman Press, 1969), p. 105.

5. Reinhold Niebuhr, *The Self and the Dramas of History* (New York: Charles Scribner's Sons, 1955), pp. 229-230.

6. Charles Schulz, *Peanuts,* United Features Syndicate, Inc., 1970.

7. C. S. Lewis, *Christian Behavior,* Book III in *Mere Christianity* (New York: The Macmillan Company, 1952), pp. 98-99.

8. *Ibid.,* p. 99.

9. John Ruskin, *Modern Painters: Of Many Things,* vol. III (New York: Merrill and Baker, n.d.) pp. 328-329.

10. Tryon Edwards, comp. *The New Dictionary of Thoughts* (Charlotte, NC: Britkin Publishing, Co., 1927), p. 265.

11. William Shakespeare, *Measure for Measure,* act II, scene 2.

12. Carl Sandburg, *Abraham Lincoln, the War Years,* vol. I (New York: Harcourt, Brace & Co., 1939), p. 323.

A Christian is a person who confesses that, amidst the manifold and confusing voices heard in the world, there is one Voice which supremely wins his full assent, uniting all his powers, intellectual and emotional, into a single pattern of self-giving. That Voice is Jesus Christ. A Christian not only believes that He was; he believes in Him with all his heart and strength and mind. Christ appears to the Christian as the one stable point or fulcrum in all the relativities of history. Once the Christian has made this primary commitment he still has perplexities, but he begins to know the joy of being used for a mighty purpose, by which his little life is dignified.

Elton Trueblood, *The Company of the Committed.*

4

The Challenge of Goodness

Blessed are those who hunger and thirst for righteousness, for they shall be satisfied (Matt. 5:6).

To a generation that utilizes calorie-free colas, sugar substitutes, diet foods, steam baths, and weight-reducing clubs, it is not easy to grasp the meaning of a Beatitude which was spoken to people who lived on the edge of starvation most of their lives. Yet, we are not totally unaware of the problem. Our television sets, news magazines, and newspapers have alerted us through words and images of swollen stomachs, gaunt faces, skeleton-thin bodies, and sad eyes that are the daily companion of many in India, Bangladesh, Ethiopia, and other sections of Africa, Asia, and Latin America. To hunger for spiritual righteousness as greatly as the starving do for food is a desire that is not often found.

Craving for Righteousness

"Blessed are they which do hunger and thirst after righteousness: for they shall be filled" (KJV). The people in Palestine, to whom Jesus directed these words, knew the meaning firsthand of hunger and thirst. A laboring man's family in Palestine ate meat only about once a week and actually often lived close to starvation. Thirst was sometimes an even greater problem since they lived in such arid country and were unable to have water readily available. They could not turn on a faucet and get running water, but they depended upon streams and wells for their water supply. On a long journey across desert country, the wind, sun, and sand could quickly destroy a person who did not have an ample supply of water bags. Hunger and thirst were daily companions for these biblical people. No afternoon snack break, iced-tea, or cola was possible to quench their hunger pangs. The need for food and drink which Jesus mentioned in this Beatitude is not to satisfy the nibbling mood of one who merely desires a snack but is focused on a craving which is essential to one's survival.

According to an ancient story, a religious prophet met a man one day who wanted to find the path to life. The prophet led him down into a river, where the man assumed he was being taken for some kind of purification ritual. Suddenly the prophet grabbed the man and thrust him under the water and held him there. After a few moments the man finally was able to free himself and came up gasping for breath. "When you thought you were drowning," the prophet then asked the man, "what did you desire most?" "Air," the man exclaimed. "When you want salvation," the prophet responded, "as much as you wanted air, then you will get it." This ancient prophet has come close to the thought which Jesus was teaching in this fourth Beatitude.

In a sense, then, this Beatitude is a challenge to us. The desire for righteousness needs to be a drive so urgent and demanding that it challenges the believer to ask himself whether he or she wants righteousness as intensely as a drowning man gasping for air, a starving child hungering for food, or a weary desert traveler dying of thirst and craving water.

Jess Carr, in his biographical novel *The Saint of the Wilderness*, relates the adventures of an itinerant mountain preacher, Robert Sayers Sheffey, as he traveled and preached throughout the hills of Virginia and West Virginia. On one occasion he decided to travel to Bluefield by the way of Wolf Creek to South Gap and then across East River Mountain. He had spent the night with a family and was up early riding along Wolf Creek, singing to himself, when suddenly he heard galloping hooves coming toward him. He guided his horse to the shoulder of the road to allow the speeding rider room to pass. Instead of passing him, however, a young rider reined in his horse and engulfed them both in a cloud of dust. "My brother, George, got bit by a rattlesnake this mornin,' " the young boy cried. "We're afraid he's goin' to die. Pa just now seen you passin' and said for me to overtake you and get you to pray for George."

"Do I know you and your family?" Robert asked him. "Your face is not familiar."

"No, you don't know us, but Pa and Ma both knows of you. Pa said if you'd pray for George the Lord would let him live."

Robert followed the boy to his home where he saw George lying on the grass in the backyard. The mother, who was attending the lad, would not allow her eyes to meet the inquiring gaze of the preacher.

"Reverend Sheffey," the father said, as he came out of the kitchen, "call upon the Lord so my boy will live."

"Have *you* ever called upon the Lord's name, my brother?" inquired Robert.

"No, but if you'll do it the Lord will surely hear our prayers. It is said that many things you pray for come to pass even after many years."

"And you have a wife and children, I see. How many? Do *they* ever call upon the name of the Lord?"

"No, I guess not," the father responded as he hung his head. "There's three boys and us."

Robert always knelt to pray on a sheepskin. "Son," he

said to the boy, "would you fetch my sheepskin from my saddle?" Before his knees were on the sheepskin, the others were already on their knees with their eyes closed. The boy who had been bitten covered his face with his hands.

> "Oh Lord," Robert prayed, "please bring Thy healing to this young man, and Lord in the same breath we thank Thee for snakes and pray that there be many of them. It is because of a snake that this family calls upon Thy holy name today. One of the sons has been bitten, and they call upon Thee. Now, Lord, get the picture: except for the snake they would perhaps never in their lifetimes have turned to Thee. What a blessing this lowly, crawling thing has been! Lord, I want you to send lots of snakes. Send another one to bite the youngest boy here, and send still another to bite this woman who never had her boys kneel by her chair, that they might hear the prayers of their mother. And, Lord, above all things, send a great big rattler, a really large one, to bite the old man so that he may call upon Thy name fervently and much. Amen."[1]

What are the pressures, obstacles, needs, desires, or burdens that eventually drive us to an awareness of our need of God? The mountain preacher saw the absence of any desire for God in the life of this family until they were crushed down by immediate danger. I saw a church sign once with this inscription on it: "When all else fails, sinners pray." Many think about God or their relationship to Him only when the going gets tough. There is no way one can see this as the greatest desire in one's life.

It is indeed difficult for us to realize that the demand which Jesus Christ makes upon every one of us as disciples is unconditional and uncompromising. In this Beatitude Jesus is challenging us to see that His way is not just for the curious, the interested bystander, or the superficial observer. Nor was He calling men and women merely to charm, delight, amuse, or entertain them. His demand was absolute. "But seek ye first the kingdom of God, and his righteousness" (Matt. 6:33, KJV). "Thou shalt love the Lord thy God with all thy heart, and with all thy soul, and with all thy mind" (22:37, KJV).

Personal Righteousness

A part of our longing for righteousness is very personal. It concerns our own conduct and behavior. Have you ever asked yourself why you would want to live a clean, moral, decent life? A conversation between Dinny and her mother in John Galsworthy's novel, *Maid in Waiting*, raises this very issue. "Providence is too remote, Mother. It's too remote," Dinny declares. "I suppose there is an eternal plan, but we are like gnats for all the care it has of us." "Don't encourage such feelings, Dinny," replies the mother, "they affect one's character." "I don't see the connection between beliefs and character," replies Dinny. "I'm not going to behave any worse because I cease to believe in Providence or in an afterlife. . . . If I'm decent it's because decency's the decent thing and not because I'm going to get anything by it." "Yes," the mother responds, "but why is decency the decent thing if there is no God?"2 Here the heart of the matter is laid open.

Right living, proper behavior, and decency, unless they are left to the mercy of every changing fad and fashion, must be anchored to something eternal, abiding, and changeless. This is the reason the Christian affirms that our standard for living is rooted in our faith in God as He has revealed Himself to us in Jesus Christ. "The law of God is like a carpenter's straightedge, and laid on his character, will enable him to see where his character deviates from rectitude."3

During the Vietnam war the term *credibility gap* was used to indicate the public disbelief in the trustworthiness of what government officials were reporting about the war. In other words, the public often believed it had been lied to by its government. After the shock of the scandal of "Watergate" and the resignation of former President Nixon, our nation was shaken at the lack of any sense of integrity in such high places of government. But integrity is often not very visible on other levels in our society either.

Misrepresentation in advertising is seen on every hand, lying is just a convenient way of conversation to get one out of a difficult situation, shoplifting is at an all-time high, cheating in schools is alarming, term-paper mills are a booming business, pilfering in offices, businesses, and factories is also on the rise. The new American code seems to be "Anything you do is OK—if you don't get caught." Is stealing no longer seen as a sin or as breaking the moral code of righteousness? The answer which many give is frightening.

Several years ago in a letter to Ann Landers, a Chicago mother wrote:

> Our 12-year-old son is selling his homework and my husband thinks it is just terrific. He keeps saying, "That kid will make it big one of these day."
>
> Albert has fixed prices (from what I gather when he talks on the telephone). He gets a dime for an arithmetic assignment and 25 cents for a book review. He bragged at dinner tonight that he has saved up $21.
>
> I think this is disgraceful but whenever I open my mouth I am shouted down. My husband insists that Albert has ingenuity, is smart, and is making his brains pay off. If I am wrong, please tell me. If my husband is wrong, please tell him. I'm beginning to doubt my own sanity.

Miss Landers' response reads:

Dear Mother: You are not wrong and I hope you'll keep talking. In this age of tax-chiseling, padded expense accounts, and political payoffs, it's no small wonder a kid would take to selling his homework. Someone should explain to the boy that it is admirable to help friends with their homework by showing them how to do it. But a person who sells "help" is supporting dishonesty in them and behaving dishonestly in them and behaving dishonestly himself.[4]

When parents encourage this kind of behavior, it is no small wonder that the situation in our society is not even worse than it is. "For a lie always harms another;" warned the philosopher Immanuel Kant, "if not some other particular man, still it harms mankind generally, for it vitiates the source of law itself."[5]

Recently a friend told me about the lack of marital fidelity which was sweeping through the office where he worked. Many of the couples were now divorced, and others flaunted their extramarital affairs before their co-workers and spoke about experiencing new "highs" in their lives. But no one spoke of this unfaithfulness as adultery. Our moral compass has been lost and each person decides for himself or herself what is right or wrong. On every hand there are reflections today of the low moral level of society. These are no longer whispers but are now shouts of defiance and perversion. Many seek only "experiments in pleasure," "anything goes," "if it feels good, do it," "nothing really matters but pleasure," "I gotta be me," "nice guys finish last," or "eat, drink, and be merry for tomorrow you die."

"Our characters," Aristotle wrote centuries ago, "are the result of our conduct."[6] One of the most foolish notions modern man has is that he can achieve high character without effort or will power. "Character, it should be noted, is to morality what being is to doing," Paul Simmons observed. "This means both that one does what one is and that one becomes what one does. Action and being affect one another."[7] Good character does not just happen; it comes about by resolving to attain it. Jesus indicated that righteousness was not acquired easily.

> Enter by the narrow gate; for the gate is wide and the way is easy, that leads to destruction, and those who enter by it are many. For the gate is narrow and the way is hard, that leads to life, and those who find it are few (Matt. 7:13-14).

A young girl told her mother, after an elderly woman friend of her mother's had left, "If I could be such an old lady as she is—so beautiful, sweet, serene, and lovable—I would not mind growing old." "Well, if you want to be that kind of an old lady," the wise mother replied, "you'd better begin now. She doesn't impress me as a piece of work that was done in a hurry." Character is something we spend our whole lives constructing. It is built stone by stone, thought by thought, response by response, word by word, deed by deed, day by day, and year by year. Each person is the architect of his or her own character and one must begin in infancy if the structure is to be stable and strong.

Our reputation is what other people say we are or what we appear to be. Reputation can be only a show or reflection of what we are really like within. Our character is what we are deep within ourselves. Our outward actions, however, often reveal the nature of our inner character. "The shortest and surest way to live with honor in the world," the Greek philosopher Socrates once observed, "is to be in reality what we would appear to be; all human virtues increase and strengthen themselves by the practice and experience of them."[8] Jesus expressed this truth about His disciples when He declared that they would be recognized by their "fruits."

> Are grapes gathered from thorns, or figs from thistles? So, every sound tree bears good fruit, but the bad tree bears evil fruit. A sound tree cannot bear evil fruit. Every tree that does not bear good fruit is cut down and thrown into the fire. Thus you will know them by their fruits (Matt. 7:17-20).

Righteousness has been defined as conformity to God's standard for right and justice. Without a correct standard, it would be impossible to determine any kind of measurement. Whether it be inches, feet, ounces, pounds, pecks, or bushels, they must be tested by standards. Washington, D. C. houses the government's Bureau of Standard Weights and Measures to make sure that the standards used in our country are correct and honest. Proper standards are essential for the transaction of business and daily living. But there are also absolutes for moral life.

Sometimes our moral standards can be misunderstood or misdirected and focused only on external or petty things. In Jesus' day righteousness was judged primarily in terms of attendance, contributions, and the obedience of certain priestly rules, precepts, laws, and traditions which had been passed along for generations. Later in the Sermon on the Mount, Jesus expands His interpretation of righteousness to caution His disciples, "Except your righteousness shall exceed the righteousness of the scribes and Pharisees, ye shall in no case enter into the kingdom of heaven" (Matt. 5:20, KJV). We often express amazement at the seemingly superficial nature of much of the religious conduct of the scribes and Pharisees, but unless we are careful we can fall into the same mistake of identifying religious conduct with the wrong standard.

One day a man was approached by his neighbor who

tried to persuade him to join his church. "Before you can join our church," he said, "you must agree to sign this statement which indicates what we believe as church members." The neighbor read the list and observed, "Your list is composed of things a person is not supposed to do." Pointing to his dog he noted, "Spot could sign that piece of paper, and it still would not make him a Christian. I can see what you folks are against, but what are you for?" His point is well taken. Granted, there are certain things which the Christian tries to refrain from, but one's basic emphasis must be on what one does and not on what one does not do.

Jesus told His disciples that they were to be the salt, the light, and the leaven in society so that "they may see your good works, and glorify your Father which is in heaven" (Matt. 5:16, KJV). Most of the rest of the Sermon on the Mount focuses on the positive ways Christians should live in society. Jesus indicated the standard for the Christian when He said, "Be ye therefore perfect, even as your Father which is in heaven is perfect" (v. 48, KJV). "But nobody is perfect," someone will argue. Jesus did not say, "Blessed are they who have attained righteousness." He stated, "Blessed are they which do hunger and thirst after righteousness" (KJV) Righteousness or perfection is not something any one of us fully achieves, but it is the goal, desire, or aim toward which we move. Our desire is always to be more Christlike. It is an ever-receding goal. The closer we come to Christ, the more we are aware that we must grow to be more like Him. But our appetite for righteousness indicates that we are, at least, on our way toward reaching for the goal.

Social Righteousness

"What has happened to our sense of integrity?" the man asked me as we were reflecting on what had been revealed to our nation about some of our political leaders in the light of the Watergate crisis. Jeb Magruder expressed the problem well when he stated to the Senate Committee, "We lost our moral compass." Our morality, Christian ethics, and righteousness have not only a personal dimension, however, but are social concerns as well. A righteous man's life is a charade if he does not attempt to bring righteousness to the institutions and society in which he lives. No one can truly live a righteous life isolated or separated from the rest of humanity. To seek righteousness is to aspire for rightness in one's personal behavior, but it is also to seek rightness in society. "The dominant values that still seem to maintain their hold over our culture," Senator Mark Hatfield noted, "are those of materialism. We still find ourselves valuing things more than other people. What we hold in our hands is far more precious to us that what we store up within our hearts."9

Sometimes we make the mistake of thinking that righteousness is merely being respectable and practicing private purity. The great prophets of Israel, such as Micah, Isaiah, Amos, Jeremiah, and others, noted the futility of Israel's worship when it focused only on ritual, animal sacrifices, or objective ceremonial rites and private morality. Amos was fierce in his denunciation of the shallowness of much of their worship. "I hate, I despise your feasts, and I take no delight in your solemn assemblies. But let justice roll down like waters, and righteousness like an ever-flowing stream" (Amos 5:21, 24). The Christian way of life is personal, but it is never depicted as private.

Someone has said that the Book of Amos is "a cry for social justice." It is a cry that demands that genuine religion be concerned for the oppressed, the poor, and all who suffer from injustice. Just as the Old Testament prophets interpreted righteousness to mean rightness in all of society, Jesus continued, reaffirmed, and strengthened that affirmation. *The New English Bible* in its translation of this Beatitude makes its meaning clearer. "How blest are those who hunger and thirst to see right prevail; they shall be satisfied." The small First Epistle of John is an expansion of the idea of putting love into social practice.

> Beloved, let us love one another: for love is of God; and every one that loveth is born of God, and knoweth God. If a man say, I love God, and hateth his brother, he is a liar: for he that loveth not his brother whom he hath seen, how can he love God whom he hath not seen (1 John 4:7, 20, KJV)?

John Killinger told the consternation of a young priest who had spent four years at Vatican II and had gone to attend a meeting of bishops and theologians in one of the comfortable hotels in Paris. Their discussion focused on the geometrical design of the pall, which is the small piece of cloth or cloth-covered cardboard that is used to cover the chalice in Mass. The learned discussion went on for days. One day there was so much noise in the street outside the hotel that one of the bishops got up from the conference table and closed the wooden shutters on the window to shut out the noise so they could concentrate better. "Do you know what that noise was?" the priest asked. "Do you know what the clatter was coming from? It was the student revolution of May 1968!" "It can hardly come as a surprise," Killinger observed," when I say that the priest is highly critical of the structures of his church and wonders how they can survive the crunch of the next few decades."[10]

In his inaugural message at His hometown synagogue in Nazareth, Jesus began His ministry linking His message of salvation with concern for the poor, enslaved, the blind and the oppressed (Luke 4:18-19). On another occasion Jesus indicated that the question God would ask us at the judgment would focus on our concern for those in need (Matt. 25:35-36). When Jesus was asked what was the greatest Commandment He listed two: We are to love God and secondly to love our neighbor. The two are joined as one. Therefore, the great social and political questions are legitimate concerns for the Christian. We cannot ignore as none of our business the great problems of war, racism and prejudice, poverty, famine, corrupt politics, the drug and alcohol crisis, gambling, pollution and ecological issues, the energy crisis, and many other social enigmas. To love or hunger for righteousness is to long for it in these areas as well as within our own personal lives. To ignore the giant social issues of our day is to be unlike our Master and leave the woman at the well, the beggar at the gate, the lame in his bed, the blind in his darkness, and the poor in his poverty. Our sense of righteousness can never be satisfied until it has a social as well as personal dimension.

Many church members, however, do not want to have to reflect on the social dimension of the gospel. They are like the man who told his pastor, "I get so tired of coming to church and hearing you talk about the problems of poverty, wars, race, pollution, and the like. I come to church to forget about those things. I want to think only about God and His holiness. You turn my thoughts away from God and toward the world. I don't like that." Although his distress may be understandable, it is a corruption of the gospel. God is not known apart from His world, but in and with it. It was, after all, for the world that Jesus came and died (John 3:16).

Walter Rauschenbusch told about a practice which health officers used in Toronto, Canada around the turn of the century to show whether milk was too dirty to be accepted. If the milk was defiled, after emptying the milk cans, large red labels were then placed on them to show that the milk in them had been too dirty to pass inspection. This way, even if the farmer didn't care about the health of those who would use the milk, the red labels served as a moral irritant because he lost the good opinion of his own neighbors and was open to their ridicule. One day a Mennonite farmer discovered his cans with the red labels on them, and he swore a worldly oath. Since the Mennonites do not even believe in swearing in court, this man was brought before his church and excluded. "But, mark well," Rauschenbusch noted, "not for introducing cow-dung into the intestines of babies, but for expressing his belief in the damnation of the wicked in a non-theological way." Rauschenbusch believed the situation could have been handled better if they had said: " 'Our brother was angry; we urged him to settle this alone with God. But he has also defiled the milk supply by unclean methods. Having the life and health of young children in his keeping, he has failed in his trust. Voted that he be excluded until he has proved his lasting repentance.' The result would be the same, but the sense of sin would do its work more intelligently."[11]

The one-cause mentality, as Ernest Campbell has observed, can always leave us uncomfortable.[12] Anyone can rally around a single emphasis and make us aware of how little we may be doing for that particular cause. What have you done lately for the David Livingstone Hospital, or the Gray Dog Society, or the South American Minister's Fund? Often this is the way we approach Christianity. We see our faith only in terms of polarities—evangelism or social action. This philosophy projects an either/or situation; if you advocate evangelism, you cannot be supportive of social action, or if you encourage social justice, you cannot be evangelistic. Who says we have to be only one-cause Christians?

Robert Raines in his book, *The Secular Congregation*, looked at this fragmented thinking in terms of the "pietist-secularist" controversy.[13] The pietist is primarily church-centered and emphasizes what God has done in the past in His mighty acts. The secularist is primarily world-centered and stresses what God is doing now in the world. The pietist prays, "Lord, change me," while the secularist prays, "Lord, change the world." Raines believed that both of these emphases are essential. Elizabeth O'Connor in the title of one of her books, *Journey Inward, Journey Outward,* noted that one emphasis without the other provides an incomplete and inadequate faith.[14] The attempt to divide our faith into "Pietist" and "Activist," Elton Trueblood declared, has resulted in a polarization. He concluded, "Service without devotion is rootless, devotion without service is fruitless."[15]

The Christian gospel is vitally concerned with both aspects of the faith. The choice is not either evangelism or social action. They are two sides of the same coin. Life is a two-directional journey. The gospel reaches inward to change my life, yet it does not end there, but it is also a journey that reaches outward to change the world. The gospel is concerned with the redemption both of persons and society. Authentic New Testament evangelism advocates not just one prong, but is concerned with both personal and social depths of the faith. The righteousness which Jesus indicates is blessed is concerned with both personal and social morality. In a vital Christian faith we seek to incorporate both phases into our living and witness.

Satisfying Our Hunger

Private morality is separated from public morality at a heavy price. The Watergate crisis is a clear case in point. "We had a private morality," Jeb Magruder stated, "but not a sense of public morality. Instead of applying our private morality to public affairs, we accepted the President's standards of political behavior, and the results were tragic for him and for us."[16] Although his book, *Moral Man and Immoral Society,* was written over forty years ago, Reinhold Niebuhr's basic theme is still correct. In his book he struggled with the kinds of forces in our society which suck individuals like Magruder into their vortex when they have not faced the awesome power of evil that often exists in a collective egoism which is much more powerful than our own individual egos.

Harold C. Phillips described the relationship of the social and personal aspects of the gospel as all one piece. He insisted that they are not like two halves of an apple, where one might cut an apple in two and eat one half and throw the other half away. The part one eats is still apple. The personal and social relationships of the gospel are more like the two sides of our hand, he observed. One cannot separate the palm of his hand from the back without destroying the hand. "Religion and ethics belong together," Phillips noted. "The 'personal' and the 'social gospel' are one and the same. Without ethical concern, religion becomes a sterile formality, an empty form. Without religion, ethics loses its meaning." "If Jesus moralized theology," he continued, "it is our task to theologize morality. If he humanized the divine, it is our task to, if I may coin a word, 'divinize' the human. Our task is to keep together what God has joined together. Only by keeping them together, can religion be saved from sterility and irrelevance and ethics from secularization if not ultimate destruction."17

In one of Nathaniel Hawthorne's stories he told about an intelligence office in a large city in which a stern figure presides over the lost-and-found records. One by one people come looking for something they have lost—such as faded beauty, influence, or a good reputation. One day a prince comes in search of a priceless jewel which he has lost carelessly in his travels. When the figure at the desk opens the cabinet, the prince sees hundreds of lost articles —wedding rings which have slipped from fingers when vows were broken, lost virginity, corrupted principles, faded youthful quests for truth, and many others. After much searching they spot the pearl and the prince exclaims, "There is my jewel! Give it to me this moment or I perish!" The intelligence officer informs the prince that he now has no more claim upon the pearl than anyone else since he once had it and then lost it. All of the prince's cries fall on unsympathetic ears, and finally he leaves without his great possession.

Life offers us opportunities to reach for the highest and the best, but when we surrender to lesser values and lower ideas, it gradually becomes difficult, if not impossible, for us to recover what we have lost by our own strength. Jesus indicated the costly nature of discipleship when He declared:

> If any one comes to me and does not hate his own father and mother and wife and children and brothers and sisters, yes even his own life, he cannot be my disciple. Whoever does not bear his own cross and come after me, cannot be my disciple. So therefore, whoever of you does not renounce all that he has cannot be my disciple (Luke 14:26-27, 33).

In this hard saying of Christ, it is evident that His way

will be demanding and difficult. Jesus never minimized His requirements for the convenience of His listeners. He wanted everyone to know that His way would often be difficult in its demands, unaccommodating in its principles, arduous in its perspective, exacting in its duration, and often perplexing to others in its injunctions. But, on the other hand, Jesus has noted that His way is the only way that brings real meaning and joy to life. "I came that they may have life, and have it abundantly" (John 10:10). "These things I have spoken to you, that my joy may be in you, and that your joy may be full" (15:11).

"Blessed are those who hunger and thirst for righteousness, for they shall be satisfied" (RSV). The King James version translates it, "they shall be filled." Here we have echoes of the familiar twenty-third Psalm where one finds "green pastures" and "still waters." In the Jewish imagery the Messianic Age was depicted as a great feast. A person can hunger and thirst after his own desires, rights, or power and get them but still be left empty. The contentment or satisfaction which comes from setting our goals on personal goodness and social justice brings a fullness and nourishment that is unknown by any other way. It is a sense of fulfillment which comes from a right relationship with God. It gives our lives purpose, meaning, and direction. Although the Christian can never claim he has fully arrived in his quest for the satisfaction of his deepest needs and the needs of mankind, he or she can affirm with the apostle Paul: "Brethren, I do not consider that I have made it my own; but one thing I do, forgetting what lies behind and straining forward to what lies ahead, I press on toward the goal for the prize of the upward call of God in Christ Jesus" (Phil. 3:13).

Notes

1. Jess Carr, *The Saint of the Wilderness* (Radford, Va: Commonwealth Press, Inc., 1974), p. 317.

2. John Galsworthy, *Maid in Waiting*, Book I. (New York: Charles Scribner's Sons, 1934), pp. 214-215.

3. John A. Broadus, *Sermons and Addresses* (New York: Eaton & Mains, 1886). p. 102.

4. Ann Landers, Publishers-Hall Syndicate, *Courier-Journal* Louisville, Ky.

5. Immanuel Kant, *Critique of Practical Reason* translated by Lewis Black (Chicago: The University of Chicago Press, 1949), p. 347.

6. Aristotle, *Nicomachean Ethics*, Book II, chapter 1.

7. Paul A. Simmons, (Editor/Contributor) *Issues in Christian Ethics* (Nashville: Broadman Press, 1980), p. 31.

8. Aristotle, *Rhetorica*, Book I, Chapter 9.

9. Mark O. Hatfield, *Conflict and Conscience* (Waco, Tex.: Word Books, 1971), p. 134.

10. John Killinger, *The Second Coming of the Church* (Nashville: Abingdon Press, 1974), pp. 9-10.

11. Walter Rauschenbusch, *A Theology for the Social Gospel* (New York: The Macmillian Co., 1917), pp. 35-36.

12. Ernest T. Campbell, *Locked in a Room with Open Doors* (Waco, Tex.: Word Books, 1974), p. 114.

13. Robert A. Raines, *The Secular Congregation* (New York: Harper & Row, 1968), p. 1ff.

14. Elizabeth O'Connor, *Journey Inward, Journey Outward* (New York: Harper & Row, 1968), p. ixff.

15. Elton Trueblood, *The New Man for Our Time* (New York: Harper & Row, 1970), p. 25.

16. *The New York Times*, May 23, 1974.

17. Harold Cooke Phillips, *The Timeless Gospel* (New York: Abingdon Press, 1956), p. 142.

Calvary is both the watershed and wellspring of history. Rightly and reverently pondered, it is the crux and the journeying Mercy of every wayfarer. It is His heart, with strong beat and red compassions, who loved us and gave Himself for us. All words are poor to tell the story of Golgotha, for words can only hint its meaning. But the words of the Book are best. They are ultimate in strength, beauty, and simple faith.

George A. Buttrick, *The Christian Fact and Modern Doubt.*

5

The Price of Mercy

Blessed are the merciful, for they shall obtain mercy. (Matt. 5:7).

The fifth Beatitude sounds so obvious. It brings to our minds images of the Red Cross, the Salvation Army, rescue missions, the ship *Hope*, the Life Saving Crew, the good Samaritan, Florence Nightingale, airlifts for the refugees and orphans of South Vietnam and other war-torn countries, and many other gracious acts done to help the needy or sick. This Beatitude does not seem as radical as the others and appeals to our sense of kindness and concern for the unfortunate. Many people teach their children the philosophy, "Be kind to others and they will be kind to you." Here is a religious word from the list of Beatitudes that is acceptable to modern society. It appears to be just good, plain, old-fashioned, common sense. But is this Beatitude as simple, or appealing, or understood, or practiced as much as we would like to believe?

The Difficulty of Being Merciful

Although this Beatitude does not seem extreme to us today, it was, nevertheless, unusual in the ancient world. Compassion was viewed negatively by the Romans and Stoics. Ruthlessness, toughness, and strength were valued virtues. Later, Nietzsche was to loathe the Christian faith and look down on it for its "slave morality." Since the traditional Jewish concepts depicted suffering as the punishment for one's sins, why should anyone attempt to change the will of God? Jesus' words, "Blessed are the merciful, for they shall obtain mercy," were more shocking to His listeners than we can imagine. While the words may not have a shrill tone to us now, are they really as easy to accept as we would like to think? Unfortunately, this Beatitude is not as simple to follow as we might believe at first glance. The act of granting mercy, for example, to someone who has hurt or wronged us, is difficult to put into practice. Forgiveness is an essential ingredient in mercy. As C. S. Lewis has noted, however, forgiveness is often an unpopular and terrible duty.

> Every one says forgiveness is a lovely idea, until they have something to forgive, as we had during the war. And then, to mention the subject at all is to be greeted with howls of anger. It is not that people think this too high and difficult a virtue: it is that they think it hateful and contemptible. "That sort of talk makes them sick," they say. And half of you already want to ask me, "I wonder how you'd feel about forgiving the Gestapo if you were a Pole or a Jew?"[1]

"I'll forgive but I won't forget" is an expression often used which indicates our unwillingness really to be merciful. I heard about a man who was dying and was afraid because of the hatred he had held against another man. He sent for the man and they made overtures of peace and shook hands in friendship. But as the visitor was leaving the sick man raised himself up and said, "Remember, if I get over this, the old quarrel stands." Genuine mercy is not easy because it demands that we surrender vindictiveness, retaliation, revenge, jealousy, and resentment. It is not enough to say, "I'll forgive but I won't let her forget" or "Oh yes, I'll forgive him, but I hope I'll never see him again." Mercy does not seek to humiliate someone, or keep him in his place, or harbor blame, or make him first crawl before you, or prove himself. Forgiveness is a form of mercy which frees the person who has wronged us by not holding the offense against him and bearing within ourselves our anger and disappointment at his actions.

One of the real difficulties with forgiveness is that often the one who has offended us does not ask for forgiveness. We have to forgive them and, at the same time, refrain from holding negative feelings or vindictive thoughts toward them. This is never easy! Forgiveness does not mean that we condone his act, but it does involve often absorbing hostility, rejection, or frustration. The death of Christ on Calvary reveals the extent of God's mercy. Merciful living then is not painless, effortless, comfortable, or tranquil. But it is the way of Christ. Forgiveness is at the heart of our faith. "I am telling you what Christianity is," Lewis declared, "I did not invent it."[2]

The costly nature of mercy was recently revealed again to me in the experience that Jay Meck, a Pennsylvania farmer, and his wife had. On a Friday afternoon in October 1974, Jay had finished his milking early and was completing some other chores because he planned to take his children to the New Holland Fair, which was always a highlight for them. He knew that soon it would be time for his young seven-year-old son, Nelson, to be getting off the school bus. His mother would always have a snack, like gingerbread, ready for him when he came in. Nelson would usually eat his snack, come by, and greet his father, and they would laugh together awhile and talk about what he did at school that day. Then he would run down the dusty road to wait for his older brother, Johnny. When his brother arrived, Nelson would always meet him with, "Ha-ha, I got home before you. What took you so long?" After their exchange they would turn and race back to the house.

Suddenly Jay was aware of a voice, but he knew it was not his son's. The bus driver shouted: "Nelson's been hit by a car! Call an ambulance!" Ruth, Jay's wife, heard the driver from the house and said she would call. With his heart pounding like a tractor in the wrong gear, Jay raced toward the highway. He saw his young son lying motionless stretched out on highway 340. He bent over and brushed back the hair from his son's face. In a choking voice he asked, "Who hit him?" After a moment of silence a young man, standing with his wife, stepped forward with a frightened and dazed look. "He just ran out in front of us," he said. Jay got up and walked toward them. Although he was not a man of violence, he was unsure what he might do. He extended his hand and said, "Jay Meck's my name." The man flinched but shook hands. Jay and Ruth followed the ambulance to the emergency room, and within a few moments, Dr. Shaw, the family physician, appeared and said, "Nelson's gone."

Jay and Ruth struggled for weeks with their grief and ache. Friends came by and poured out their sympathy. Later, as they learned that the man who had hit their son was an off-duty New York City policeman, it only served to compound the accident and make it seem even more senseless. Of all people, they felt, he should know to stop for the flashing lights of a school bus. His neighbors did not help these feelings when they would say: "I sure hope that guy gets all that's coming to him;" or "You're going to throw the book at him, aren't you?" A few week after Nelson's funeral, the insurance adjuster came by to talk about the accident. In the course of the conversation, the other couple was mentioned and Jay and Ruth asked if they could meet them. The couple accepted an invitation to come to the Meck's home for a meal. Ruth and Jay prayed as the day grew closer that they would have strength and guidance to meet them. As they talked that day, Jay said a strange feeling of compassion toward them began to come over him. Frank, the policeman, had an eight-year spotless record, but this accident might cost him his job. Frank, his wife, and their three children had moved in with his wife's parents because they could not face their neighbors.

At dinner the conversation turned to a discussion about church. Ruth indicated that she and her husband were Sunday School teachers at their local Mennonite church. "But it's more than a church," Ruth said. "You've really got to live out your beliefs every day." After the couple left, Jay and Ruth began to reflect on their grief in the light of their understanding that faith is to be lived out every day. They came to the conclusion that hatred or vengeance was not the solution to a mistake someone else had made. As they sought to employ the kind of love which Jesus stood for they reached out to this other couple with compassion and did not press charges at the trial. "No matter how deep the wound of sorrow is," Jay observed, "forgiveness and faith in God will provide the strength. . . . and the broken pieces of our lives will be made whole in Him."[3] No one can say that this action was easy, but it certainly was in the spirit of the one who said, "Blessed are the merciful, for they shall obtain mercy."

The Quality of Mercy

Mercy is a rich biblical word. The Hebrew word for *mercy* occurs more than one-hundred-and-fifty times in the Old Testament. This word has been translated *to have compassion, to pity, to be gracious, to spare,* or simply as *mercy, kindness, loving-kindness,* or *steadfast love.* God's mercy for Israel was based on the covenant which He had made with them. Mercy is the steadfast and faithful characteristic of God's relationship with humanity. "My mercy will I keep for him for evermore, and my covenant shall stand fast with him" (Ps. 89:28, KJV). His loving-kindness was evident in His deliverance of Israel from Egypt, in His many provisions, in His sustaining love, and in His forgiveness. God's mercy was seen as the source of a person's strength, assurance, hope, peace, comfort, and trust (Isa. 54:8; 49:10; Ps. 6:4; Num. 14:18-19; Pss. 33:18; 40:11). Mercy, in the Old Testament view, was not depicted as something persons deserved or as something which was God's duty to render. It was God's gracious response based on His outpouring love, and He expected this same type of response from persons in their relationships with each other (Mic. 6:8; Hos. 6:6).

In his novel *Love Is Eternal,* Irving Stone gave a narrative account of a conversation between Mary Todd, the wife of Abraham Lincoln, and Parker, the President's bodyguard. Parker, a heavy-faced man with half-closed eyes, entered and trembled before Mrs. Lincoln.

"Why were you not at the door to keep the assassin out?" she asked fiercely.

"I have bitterly repented it," Parker answered, his head hung low. "But I did not believe that anyone would try to kill so good a man in such a public place. The belief made me careless. I was attracted by the play, and did not see the assassin enter the box."

"You should have seen him." Falling back on the pillow, she covered her face with her hands. "Go now. It's not you I can't forgive, it's the assassin."

"If Pa had lived," Tad, the son, said, "he would have forgiven the man who shot him. Pa forgave everybody."[4]

William Barclay has described the Hebrew word for *mercy* as "the ability to get right inside the other person's skin until we can see things with his eyes, think things with his mind and feel things with his feelings."[5] In Jesus Christ, God came into the world and identified with men and women in their struggles and sorrows. In Him we see the extent and power of the outpouring of God's mercy and love. The cry that went out to Jesus wherever He went was "Lord, have mercy." The New Testament describes Jesus as being moved with compassion toward them (Matt. 9:36; Mark 8:2; Luke 7:13). Jesus showed mercy to the blind (Matt. 20:34), the lepers (Luke 17:13), the hungry (Mark 8:2), the ignorant (Mark 6:34), the lame and sick (John 5:2-9; Mark 5:25-29). The most caustic words Jesus used were directed against the Scribes and Pharisees who emphasized the significance of the smallest detail of the law but were unwilling to practice mercy (Matt. 23:23).

The lesson from the parable of the good Samaritan shows the power of love in action (Luke 10:30-37). The parable of the unmerciful servant (Matt. 18:21-35) is the story of a man who has been forgiven a great debt but refuses himself to forgive a lesser debt which was owed to him. Jesus noted the terrible nature of mercilessness in the picture of the punishment which is given to this servant. Mercilessness is a terrible act not merely against another person, but it is also an act against a loving God.

In the account of the woman who was caught in the act of adultery and brought before Jesus to be stoned, we see the mercy of God made visible in Jesus. Without condoning her sin, Jesus challenged the crowd and asked that those who had committed no acts of sin of their own be the first to throw stones at her. When none were willing to make this kind of acknowledgment, Jesus expressed the mercy of God when He declared: "Neither do I condemn thee: go, and sin no more" (John 8:11, KJV). Here they saw the mercy of God incarnated before them. In this act of forgiveness we can see a concrete example of how Jesus hated the sin but not the sinner. Here is justice tempered with compassion. Even in His final moments, Jesus proclaimed His mercy when He cried, "Father, forgive them; for they know not what they do" (Luke 23:34).

In the novel, *The Brothers Karamazov,* Dostoevski told about a peasant woman who had fears about feeling forgiven by God. "There is no sin," the elder responds, "and there can be no sins on all the earth, which the Lord will not forgive to the truly repentant. Man cannot commit a sin so great as to exhaust the infinite love of God. . . . Believe that God loves you as you cannot conceive; that He loves you with your sin, in your sin." Quietly he continued, "If I, a sinner, even as you are, am tender with you and have pity on you, how much more will God."[6] The miracle of mercy is that a holy and righteous God extends His boundless love toward us while we are yet sinners and draws us to Himself. Such everlasting love is beyond our understanding, but it is the biblical affirmation about the very nature of God Himself.

Mercy in Action

In order to be merciful we must be empathic. Empathy is the capacity to participate in another person's feelings or ideas. It is to suffer with them, ache with them, bleed with them, struggle with them, reach out with them, cry with them, care with them, hope and dream with them. Empathy is attempting to get inside another person's skin to see life from his perspective. The word *sympathy* is derived from two Greek words which mean "to experience" or "together with." A truly sympathetic person is one who "experiences something together with" another person. He is not just an observer but is involved with another's problems or difficulties. How often, too late, do we cry, "Oh, if I had only known. . . ." Our judgments are sometimes formed too quickly, with inadequate information, limited awareness, and with strained feelings. To be merciful requires the ability to feel or suffer with the one who is affected as though you could see the situation through his or her eyes.

Christian mercy does not say casually, "Oh, it doesn't matter. Let bygones be bygones." Mercy is not merely making excuses for someone's behavior or making allowances for their strange actions. It is not winking at somebody's faults, habits, or sins. We must always be aware of the costly nature of mercy or it becomes spineless, sentimental, and insipid. Acts of mercy cannot be merely emotional responses to individuals, but in order to avoid havoc in society, they must also contain understanding, insight, love, restraint, and patience. I heard a man say once, "God will forgive me, that's His job." Yes, God is in the "forgiving business," but He is not a senile elderly father who doesn't take our sins seriously. The costly nature of God's mercy is revealed in the cross of Christ. No grace can be cheap which cost God this price.

We, too, experience the price of mercy when someone has injured us. In an effort to erase our memory and respond graciously to them, we become aware that complete forgiveness will be the costliest thing we have ever done. The costly form of mercy may take many shapes. A husband indicates to his wife that he has committed an act of indiscretion and asks for her forgiveness. They love each other very much, and yet they are aware that the wife's forgiveness and the husband's confession are costly to both of them. Both are acutely conscious of his sin, but they want to rebuild their marriage, and it cannot be done without the release of forgiveness. A friend may have hurt you with some unkind words which he related about you. He approaches you and apologizes for his action. Your forgiveness of him is not an easy act for either of you. But you both know that it is the only bridge back for reestablishing your friendship.

Your son experiments with drugs and is caught by the

authorities. He is deeply aware of how foolish he has been and genuinely desires to have another chance. As a parent and a son, trust can never exist between you again without the words, "We forgive you, let's start a new slate." But the price tag on this kind of act for both parties is high. It requires love, guidance, understanding, and faith. An employee fails to do an assignment he was given and as his employer you confront him with this omission. He acknowledges his negligence but asks for another opportunity to prove himself. In your decision you evaluate your business and your employee's potential future, aware that your forgiveness can help or hurt your business or a young man.

Several years ago one of my church families was driving home from the store when another car ran a red light and killed the wife instantly and put the husband in the intensive-care unit of the hospital. Later, after the husband had improved, he and his children talked with the young woman who had driven the other car. She had become deeply depressed over the accident, although it was something she could not help since her accelerator had stuck and she was not able to dislodge it. When they met the young woman, the father and his children assured her that they did not blame her nor hold hard feelings toward her because of the accident. Through their understanding love, they reached out with healing to another even in the midst of their own grief. But it was not done easily.

Mercy in action is always costly. It demands that we care enough to give time, money, energy, support, encouragement, and love to those who need it. Mercy may take the form of a gracious word, a reassuring handshake, a loving embrace, a visit, a check, a smile, or many other shapes. Mercy in action is seeing a need, feeling it, and responding in understanding love. It does not focus on the cost as on the need. It refuses to yield to the hardness of the act of mercy but concentrates on the redemptive, healing power of forgiveness.

An Inescapable Principle

The fifth Beatitude is similar to the fifth petition of the Lord's Prayer which is the only petition with a condition attached to it. This Beatitude concludes with a promise. "Blessed are the merciful, for they shall obtain mercy." Jesus is not appealing to a reward motive in this teaching. This is not tit-for-tat or some kind of bargain arrangement between persons or between humankind and God. Mercy is not something we can earn. It is not a means to win God's favor or bribe Him. Jesus is not teaching that if I am merciful to Mr. Jones then Mr. Smith or Mr. Jackson will in turn be merciful to me. Life reveals that this is not always the case. Sometimes even the most merciful and forgiving people are met with meanness, ingratitude, crudeness, brutality, hardness, or ruthlessness. Jesus, who had shown so much mercy to others, was Himself rejected, betrayed, condemned, beaten, and crucified. We do not act mercifully because we expect others to respond to us in the same way, but because it is a fundamental principle written into human relationships by God Himself.

The mercy we receive is from God, not people. The unmerciful person is simply not conditioned to receive God's forgiveness. "If ye forgive men their trespasses, your heavenly Father will also forgive you: But if ye forgive not men their trespasses, neither will your Father forgive your trespasses" (Matt. 6:14-15, KJV). "With what judgment ye judge, ye shall be judged: and with what measure ye mete, it shall be measured to you again" (7:2, KJV). When Peter asked Jesus, "Lord, how often shall my brother sin against me, and I forgive him? As many as seven times?" Jesus replied, "I do not say to you seven times, but seventy times seven" (18:21-22). Forgiveness is not measured mathematically but is without limit in its scope.

A cardinal New Testament teaching is that receiving is connected to giving, that to be forgiven we must be forgiving. An unforgiving spirit closes the door against God who is always seeking to forgive us. Forgiveness can enter a life only as it is open to the mercy of God. Revenge, bitterness, hatred, or resentment toward another blocks the avenue of our own forgiveness. Our unforgiving attitude then is the factor that causes us to miss forgiveness. We revoke our right to share in God's family when we refuse to forgive the other members of the household. As Frank Stagg has observed, this is not an arbitrary requirement which Jesus set up so we could receive mercy. "It is rather that in the nature of mercy and forgiveness there cannot be receiving without giving. . . . That in one which renders him incapable of being merciful or forgiving also renders him incapable of receiving mercy or forgiveness."[7] Jesus concluded the parable of the unmerciful servant by declaring, "So likewise shall my heavenly Father do also unto you, if ye from your heart forgive not every one his brother their trespasses (Matt. 18:35, KJV). James stated that same truth this way: "He shall have judgment without mercy, that hath shewed no mercy" (Jas. 2:13, KJV).

John Wesley once had a man declare to him, "I never forgive." "Then," Wesley replied, "I hope you never offend." But we all do acts that hurt others in large or small ways. We desire forgiveness from them and God. So in turn we must learn to forgive others as we expect them to do of us and as we desire from God. To do otherwise is to cut ourselves off from our own forgiveness. Our attitude cannot be like the response of a wife to her husband after they had had a quarrel. "Come on now," he said, "I thought you had agreed to forgive and forget." "Sure," she replied, "but I don't want you to forget that I have forgiven and forgotten." The Gospel of Luke puts the qualifying phrase in the Lord's prayer in a positive way. "Forgive us our sins; for we also forgive every one that is indebted to us" (Luke 11:4, KJV).

J. Wallace Hamilton tells the story of Dr. A. J. Cronin, who was a physician for many years in England.[8] One day a young boy was brought to the hospital desperately ill with diphtheria. A tube was inserted into his throat so he could breathe and a nurse was stationed to see that the tube remained clear. Unfortunately, she dozed off and awakened to find that the tube was blocked with membrane. Instead of cleaning the tube she panicked and hysterically called the doctor out of sleep. When he got to the child's side, it was too late. The doctor was outraged that a child should die so needlessly and wrote out his report demanding her immediate expulsion. He called her in and read, his voice trembling with resentment, what he had written to the board of health. She stood before him in silence almost fainting with shame and remorse. "Well, have you nothing to say for yourself?" he asked. Only silence then in a stammering plea. "Give me . . . give me another chance."

The doctor was shocked. She had failed at her responsibility and there was nothing else to do, as he saw it. He told her to leave, sealed his report, and retired to bed, but he was unable to sleep. A far-off word floated in and continued to whisper: "Forgive us our trespasses. . . ." The next morning he tore up the report and gave her another chance. Later that young nurse became the head of a large hospital and one of the most honored nurses in England.

Mercy gives one the opportunity to begin again. Mercy is not merely sentiment; it is the word which says: "You are not finished! Try again." It is the word of hope, opportunity to begin again. It is the word of hope, encouragement, renewal, and fresh beginning. It is a word we all need to hear again and again, and a word we need to express to others again and again.

Try an experiment. Write on a piece of paper some offenses others have done to you which have hurt you deeply. After you have finished writing them down, bow for a moment and have a period of silent prayer. In this prayer forgive those who have wronged you. After the prayer is concluded, then, tear the pieces of paper into tiny pieces and throw them away. Take another piece of paper and write on it ways you have hurt others. Pray for forgiveness and, then, tear this paper up also. Pray that God will give you the strength to carry out these prayers. As you ask for mercy, learn to grant it to others.

In this Beatitude Jesus has given to us a promise and a warning. He has observed that we have the assurance of God's mercy if we are merciful. An unmerciful attitude on our part obstructs God's efforts to be merciful to us. Hindered by our own unforgiving spirit, we cannot receive our own forgiveness. When loving kindness reaches out from us to others around us who are in need or have offended us, then we have opened ourselves not only to our neighbors but to the Spirit of God. The greatness of the gospel is that God's mercy is "from everlasting to everlasting" and it is infinite and as vast as the ocean. Although we cannot earn God's mercy, He freely gives it to all who are open and receptive to it.

Shakespeare noted the benediction of the merciful:

> The quality of mercy is not strained,
> It droppeth as the gentle rain from heaven
> Upon the place beneath: it is twice blessed;
> It blesseth him that gives and him that takes:[9]

Notes

1. C. S. Lewis, *Mere Christianity* (New York: The Macmillan Company, 1943), p. 89, book III.

2. *Ibid.*

3. Jay Meck, "The Peace We Found in Forgiveness" *Guideposts*, (Carmel, N.Y.: Guideposts Associates, Inc., October 1975), pp. 1-7.

4. Irving Stone, *Love Is Eternal* (New York: Doubleday & Company, Inc., 1954), p. 459.

5. William Barclay, *The Gospel of Matthew*, vol. I (Philadelphia: The Westminster Press, 1958), p. 98.

6. Fedor Dostoevski, *The Brothers Karamazov*, (Garden City, N.Y.: International Collectors Library, n.d.), pp. 44-45.

7. Frank Stagg, Commentary on Matthew in *The Broadman Bible Commentary*, vol. 8 (Nashville: Broadman Press, 1969), p. 105.

8. J. Wallace Hamilton, *Horns and Halos in Human Nature* (New York: Fleming H. Revell Company, 1954), pp. 94-95.

9. William Shakespeare, *The Merchant of Venice*, act IV, scene I.

As far as my experience goes, I can say one thing without fear of contradiction; nothing in the world is so enheartening; nothing so quickly banishes that dark mood we call loneliness, than the response of those whom we succeed, however simply, in helping along the way. Here the words of Christ are once more so amazingly true: "He that loveth his life, loseth it. He that loseth it for My sake, shall find it unto life eternal." Shall find LIFE! The thing we are all looking for! Fullness of LIFE. Let me translate the wonderful words differently: "He who hugs life to himself, loses all joy in living, is lonely and self-excluded from joy. He who gives himself away to others shall find a fullness of life that will develop into the wholly satisfying life that is everlasting."

—Leslie D. Weatherhead, *Key Next Door.*

6

An Undivided Aim

Blessed are the pure in heart, for they shall see God
(Matt. 5:8).

Vision is a natural sense which we simply take for granted unless we are threatened with its loss. I remember visiting a lady a few years ago who was nearly blind because she had cataracts on her eyes and her vision had gradually narrowed to a tiny point of light. For years she had struggled alone in the semidarkness. After an operation, her vision was restored and once again she was able to live normally. The ability to see is one of our most valuable senses. In this Beatitude Jesus promises us sight which surpasses our fondest hopes—to be able to see God. "Blessed are the pure in heart for they shall see God" (Matt. 5:8).

Religious Purity

The appeal to see God, however, appears to be inaccessible because of the demand for inner purity. Jesus has stated that it is the pure in heart who will see God. What does it mean to be pure in heart? In speaking of the pure in heart, Jesus was seeking to break through the concept which identified purity primarily as ceremonial or the observance of certain rituals. This tended to make purity an external matter and not internal. In this usage purity is concerned with the kinds of foods and animals one might eat, with the way one should wash one's hands, with

119

other taboos and regulations regarding dress, table customs, bathing, etc. The word *pure* in Greek and Hebrew has been translated in several ways. It may mean *clean, simple, clear, without alloy, without blemish, unadulterated, unmixed,* or *single.* In the Bible the word might refer to pure water, flawless glass, unmixed oil, physically unblemished animals, family lineage, clean linen, virgin gold, and many others. Unfortunately many equated external cleanliness with religious purity. In this Beatitude Jesus offers a radical challenge to the conventional and orthodox concepts of what constitutes religious cleanness. Jesus was aware that a man could be ceremonially clean externally and at the same time hold feelings of hatred, anger, vindictiveness, pride, arrogance, or thoughts which were unwholesome, unclean, impure, dirty, unchaste, and obscene. Jesus argued that even if the outward act was performed with meticulous care, a person might still be defiled if his inner thoughts were not clean and wholesome. Jesus' concern was with what was inside a person and not merely with a clean exterior. Some of the strongest words of condemnation Jesus ever spoke were directed against ritualistic observances.

> Woe unto you, scribes and Pharisees, hypocrites! for ye make clean the outside of the cup and of the platter, but within they are full of extortion and excess. Thou blind Pharisee, cleanse first that which is within the cup and platter, that the outside of them may be clean also. Woe unto you, scribes and Pharisees, hypocrites! for ye are like unto whited sepulchres, which indeed appear beautiful outward, but are within full of dead men's bones, and of all uncleanness. Even so ye also outwardly appear righteous unto men, but within ye are full of hypocrisy and iniquity (Matt. 23:25-28, KJV).

The pure in heart then are not those who focus on

religious ceremonies, but are those who direct their mind to a single, undivided aim. Dr. John A. Hutton, who was for many years the editor of the *British Weekly,* told about the dictatorial way many of the caddies serve on the golf links at St. Andrew's in Scotland. The caddie hands a golfer the proper club, tells him the direction toward which he is to swing, and then watches the performance in silence. On one occasion a stranger, who was not familiar with the dictatorial manner of the local caddies, was preparing to tee off for a dogleg hole which had to be approached indirectly. The caddie handed the golfer a club and said, "Shoot toward that tar-roofed shed, away there to the left." "Would it not be better," observed the stranger, "to go straight for it?" "You may play in any direction you like," the caddie noted. "I was only suggesting how to play in order to win the hole."[1]

Often we feel that we can guide our own lives without any need of divine direction or guidance. So we aim our life toward the pursuit of material possessions, recreation, recognition, knowledge, or power. No room is reserved for God, or, if there is a place, it is the leftovers of our time and attention. Jesus has warned us that if we aim straight for all of the other things of life we shall miss them. Something else requires first place. "Seek ye *first* the kingdom of God, . . . and all these things shall be added" (Matt. 6:33, KJV).

All of the biblical meanings of the word *purity* convey a common thought. It is a description of something which is untainted or unmixed. *Pure in heart* is not a reference to sinlessness; instead, it describes one whose thoughts, desires, or purposes are undivided, unmixed, and genuine. It is demanding in its claim upon us, because it requires from us the concentration of our total self. The title of a book by the Danish theologian Sren Kierkegaard has expressed well the teaching of this Beatitude: *Purity of*

Heart Is to Will One Thing. This claim challenges us to examine our motives, to look inwardly, to perform an introspective examination, to be ruthlessly honest with our intentions, and to bring our total life under the purpose of Christ.

Unfortunately we are tempted to be chameleon characters in our response to life instead of learning to focus our lives in a united direction. Willa Cather, in a letter to the literary critic Maxwell Geismar, stressed the weakness of a "double-minded" attitude. "Listen, my friend, no man can give himself heart and soul to one thing while in the back of his mind he cherishes a desire, a secret hope for something very different."[2] But for many of us there is a nagging desire for something, for something not yet realized, for something we dare not disclose. We may often pretend that God has first place but underneath we know that some other motive constrains us forward. Gerald Kennedy has observed that our day is a difficult time for a single-mindedness, but he noted:

> If the Christian faith can create spirits which know unity in the midst of chaos, it is a sure sign of its eternal validity. . . . Instead of complaining about the difficulties, let us thank God that He had given us a task which commands our whole heart, our complete mind, and our entire strength.[3]

Later in the Sermon on the Mount, Jesus expressed it this way: "The light of the body is the eye: if therefore thine eye be single, thy whole body shall be full of light" (Matt. 6:22).

In Margaret Mitchell's Pulitzer-prize-winning novel, *Gone with the Wind,* Will Benteen, who had held off the Yankees, the carpetbaggers, and the encroachment of nature to save the plantation, Tara, during the Civil War, stands beside the grave of the owner, Gerald O'Hara, and eulogizes him by declaring that there wasn't anything "from the outside" that could lick him.

He warn't scared of the English government when they wanted to hang him. He just lit out and left home. And when he come to this country and was pore that didn't scare him a mite neither. He went to work and he made his money. And he warn't scared to tackle this section when it was part wild and the Injuns had just been run out of it. He made a big plantation out of a wilderness. And when the war come on and his money begun to go, he warn't scared to be pore again. And when the Yankees come through Tara and might of burnt him out or killed him, he warn't fazed a bit and he warn't licked neither. He just planted his front feet and stood his ground. That's why I say he had our good points. There ain't nothing *from the outside* can lick any of us. . . .

And I don't want none of you to think the less of him for breakin' like he done. All you all and me, too, are like him. We got the same weakness and failin'. There ain't nothin' that walks can lick us, any more than it could lick him, not Yankees nor Carpetbaggers nor hard times or high taxes nor even downright starvation. But that weakness that's in our hearts can lick us in the time it takes to bat your eye.[4]

If we are honest with ourselves, it is usually not the pressures and temptations which we meet externally that cause us the most difficulty. Our primary weakness is something internal. If we are not strong within, then we collapse and are destroyed by the storms that beat upon us. Pressures pull at the center of our being as though they would rip us apart. At moments we feel like we are going to "fall apart," "lose our cool," "come unglued," "lose control," "go to pieces," or be "tied up in a knot." Until our inner self is under control, we cannot meet the temptations, difficulties, or adversities of life constructively. Without strength from within, we will be overwhelmed by every temptation, subdued by every difficulty, defeated by every failure, and submerged by every calamity. The inner person must be fortified to resist the pressures and demands of life. This was Paul's prayer for the Ephesians:

> For this reason I bow my knees before the Father, . . . that according to the riches of his glory he may grant you to be strengthened with might through his Spirit in the inner man and that Christ may dwell in your hearts through faith (Eph. 3:14-17).

I can still see the woman as she sat before me sobbing. "One more burden, one more problem, and I'll fall to pieces," she exclaimed. "I've got to have help, or I'll never make it." She is not alone in that need. We all must have strength from within to help us bear the load, meet the strain, and stand the testing. Paul encouraged the Christian:

> Therefore take the whole armor of God, that you may be able to withstand in the evil day, and having done all, to stand. Stand therefore, having girded your loins with truth, and having put on the breastplate of righteousness, and having shod your feet with the equipment of the gospel of peace; besides all these taking the shield of faith, with which you can quench all the flaming darts of the evil one. And take the helmet of salvation, and the sword of the Spirit, which is the word of God (Eph. 6:13-17).

It is easy for us to condemn the ceremonial practices of purity rites and say that that is not our problem today. Although our external practices may have taken different forms, they can be just as wooden or artificial. Sometimes we measure a person's spirituality by his church attendance, the size of his contribution, his involvement in our church programs, or by his respectability in our community. A person may do all of these things and still have thoughts and desires which are wholly unacceptable to God. This is not to say that one should not do these things, but it is to observe that we may do them for the wrong reason or with dishonorable motives.

I heard recently of a wealthy man who was an avid church leader and a noted community worker. He had on several occasions been recognized and honored for his church and community activities. But, at the same time he was being honored for his charitable work, he was the owner of a local hotel which was known notoriously as a place of prostitution. This man evidently did not see anything incongruous in being a church leader and owning a "red-light" hotel. This is the kind of hypocrisy which Jesus denounced so vocally in many of His teachings. Can a person claim that she has high moral standards and values and be deceitful and fraudulent in her business life? This sort of duplicity of character shatters the "singlemindedness" to which Jesus is seeking to lead us. Speaking of His disciples Jesus observed, "You will know them by their fruits" (Matt. 7:16). In the small Epistle of James, the argument for the inability of separating faith or religion from one's works or daily living is forcefully concluded with the insights, "For as the body apart from the spirit is dead, so faith apart from works is dead" (Jas. 2:26).

Several years ago when a church I was pastoring was looking for an assistant minister, I received the following letter of reference from one of the young man's former college professors. "There is something wonderfully clean about the young man, and the reference there is to his mind as well as to his physical being. He is unfailingly a gentleman. . . . He is loyal to the very highest ideals, and he has both the intelligence and the character to render estimable service to those ideals. I believe that if there is one word that summarizes his many splendid qualities, it is *integrity,* and I like to think of the relationship of that word to *integer.* He is a 'whole number,' solid and sound and unblemished." Obviously, we called him. Here is a description of the pure in heart; he is clean, whole, solid, sound, and unblemished.

Inner Integrity

Today the heart is thought of primarily as a physical muscle which functions as a pumping station within our body for the circulation of blood. Heart transplants and the number-one national health problem of heart attacks are constant news items. The heart also remains our symbol for romance, and it is given and received in many shapes and forms on Valentine's Day to carry on the tradition of lovers, both young and old. But in the biblical usage, the heart represents much more than a physical organ or a romantic symbol. In ancient Hebrew thought the heart was the center of personality. They did not make sharp distinctions between the mental and physical functions of the human body and consequently they often attributed emotional, intellectual, and volitional powers to certain organs of the body.

These same concepts are evident in the New Testament as well. When Jesus refered to the pure in heart, His hearers were aware that He was not talking about a physical part of the human body, but that He was referring to the central seat of a person's life. The heart represents the whole inner self of a person. To use a modern term, the heart is basically equivalent to what we call "personality" today.

In biblical usage, it is with the heart that a person is happy, generous, loving, or envious, mean, fearful, or discouraged (Prov. 27:11; Isa. 35:4; Deut. 13:3; Num. 32:7). From the heart a person thinks, wills, and responds to God

(Ps. 4:4; Mark 2:6; Prov. 6:18; Zech. 7:12; Ps. 27:8; Rom. 10:10). God says to Israel, "And I will give them one heart, and I will put a new spirit within you; and I will take the stony heart out of their flesh, and will give them an heart of flesh" (Ezek. 11:19, KJV). Paul pictured the heart as a person's center of faith. "That if, . . . thou shalt be saved. For with the heart man believeth unto righteousness; and with the mouth confession is made unto salvation" (Rom. 10:9-10, KJV).

Sometimes we Christians sing about the wonderful change Jesus has made in our hearts. The change that Christ brings into our lives may be seen externally by the way we live and act, but the original conversion in our lives is an inward act. Christ gives us a "new heart." Now our thoughts, feelings, desires, and drives are conditioned and directed by our new Master. When Christ enters the heart of our lives, we surrender to Him our total personality and seek to follow Him and to make His way our way. We strive to say with Paul: "For me to live is Christ" (Phil. 1:21). "I am crucified with Christ: nevertheless I live; yet not I, but Christ liveth in me" (Gal. 2:20, KJV). The pure in heart have found the singleness of life's purpose fulfilled in Jesus Christ. When we follow Him, our scattered aims and mixed objectives have a sense of integration, wholeness, and holiness through His power. With Christ at the center of our lives, control and power are ours because of the new center He brings into our lives (2 Cor. 5:17).

His presence seeks to establish within us a "heart of integrity" which centuries before God had promised to King Solomon (1 Kings 9:4). Sometimes the pure in heart have to stand alone for what they believe is right. In 1868 Senator Edmund G. Ross of Kansas went through an agonizing experience in the impeachment proceedings against President Andrew Johnson. Ross had the only uncommitted vote in the Senate, and it was needed to impeach the President. His fellow senators and constituents back home all urged him to cast his vote in favor of impeachment. However, when he chose to follow his own conscience, and voted against impeachment, his decision for personal integrity was costly. He was never elected again in Kansas, and his family became social outcasts. Nevertheless, before his death in 1907 a once cruel society began to recognize the courage and integrity of this rejected man, and he is now openly praised and admired for his stand. His position was no easy one. It took courage, and the willingness to accept rejection, opposition, and hostility. But he was able to take his stand because of his own personal integrity.

We all admire this kind of courage, and wonder if we would have it if the circumstances demanded it. We would like to think so, but it is difficult to know until we are tested in the public arena. It is always easy to stand at a distance, apart from the situation, and say what another should do or have done. But it is always radically different to be in a possibly compromising situation and do the right thing for the proper reason. We need inner strength to meet the occasion.

Sir Thomas More, as presented in Robert Bolt's play, *A Man for All Seasons,* was another man of integrity. Henry VIII had imprisoned him because More had refused to compromise his beliefs and yield to the demand of the King to grant him an annulment from his marriage to the Spanish princess, Catherine of Avagon. Shut up in the prison tower and awaiting execution unless he agreed to swear to the "Act of Succession," which declares the King's marriage to Catherine as unlawful, his daughter, Margaret came to him and pleaded with him to save his life by signing the document. She reminded her father that he had taught her that God took more note of a man's inner thoughts than his spoken words. Margaret argued that More should say the required oath but repudiate it silently in his heart.

More replied that a man's oath was like trying to hold water in his hands. To open his fingers was to lose the water; to violate his oath was to lose his integrity. More chose not to be that kind of man.[5]

Here is integrity at its highest and brightest. Here is the willingness to die for right rather than violate one's conscience. More was indeed correct. Few persons are capable, or so it seems, of such acts of moral soundness. Why? Is not a part of the answer found in the absence of the inner strength necessary to sustain us in this moment of testing?

A phrase which is thrown around rather loosely when describing another person's motives is the one which depicts him or her as being either sincere or insincere. Insincerity is a harsh criticism while sincerity is a lofty demand. Consider the origin of the word *sincere*. In the Greco-Roman world marble pillars were often found with flaws in some of them. Unscrupulous sellers filled the cavities with wax and polished over them so the wax blended in with the rest of the marble, and they were sold as sound. When the impact of the natural elements beat upon them, the wax eroded away and the flaws were revealed. These pillars were not *sine cera*. They were not *without wax*. When we sign a letter and say I am "sincerely yours," we are declaring that we are "without wax." We are what we claim to be. To be sincere is to be real, genuine, unvarnished, pure, unalloyed, or unmixed. The pure in heart are sincere; they are without wax.

It is, of course, easy to sign a letter "Sincerely yours," but it is much more difficult to let our words on paper or in sound harmonize with our life. True sincerity is not merely an exercise to persuade someone else that we are honest and noble. Genuine sincerity arises out of a life filled with conviction and integrity. It is a living thing that emerges out of who we are deep within. Sincerity, if it is real, pervades a person's whole being and is the foundation of one's character. To be sincere is to reveal a sound character. Insincerity exposes a disfigurement within which no external pretense can long disguise.

For thirty-five days General William P. Dean wandered the Korean hills until he was captured on July 22, 1950. With almost no food to sustain him, he had nearly starved and was close to death when he was taken prisoner. Thinking that death was imminent, his captors allowed him to write a letter home. He thought that this was going to be his last communication with his family; however, he survived his ordeal and was released three years later in September, 1953. In his tender letter he expressed appreciation to his wife, Mildred, for their twenty-four years of happy married life, and he encouraged his daughter, June, to make her mother a grandmother soon. "Bill," he then wrote to his son, "remember that integrity is the most important thing of all. Let that always be your aim."[6]

Corrective Vision

There is more than one way of seeing. You may be shopping with your husband and he stops you and says, "Look at that dress over there; do you see it? Isn't it lovely?" You turn, look and reply, "Yes, I see it. It really is nice." That is physical vision. As a parent you are struggling with your daughter trying to help her understand a science project or a math problem. Her blank face suddenly lights up, and she shouts, "I've got it; I see it! It's so simple!" That is mental vision. John and Mary have recently become engaged. They have been "seeing" each other for years. That is love's vision. A young college student sat in my office and described her difficulty in finding a meaningful faith. We continued to talk on several occasions. She read, listened, and worshiped. Finally, one Sunday morning she came forward and said, "I have seen the light now. Jesus is real to me. I am ready to commit my life to Him." That is spiritual vision. Learning to see life in its many dimensions and responding to it are essential if we are to experience the greatness of it.

A part of the truth in this Beatitude might be expressed this way. "Blessed are the pure in heart: for they shall see." How blind even the sharpest eyes among us often are. Many animals and birds are conditioned to see much better than human beings. Charles Schulz in his "Peanuts" comic strip showed Snoopy and his bird friend, Woodstock, sitting on top of a doghouse. Snoopy said, "Woodstock has never seen a violin or a fire truck or a candy store. He's never heard an opera or a symphony . . . . He's never seen a movie or a play. . . . On the other hand, he's seen the sky, the clouds, the ground, the sun, the rain, the moon, the stars, a cat and several worms." He concluded: "Woodstock feels that he's led a very full life.[7] He has seen a great deal and often much that we miss.

Although we are surrounded by miracles daily, we simply do not take the trouble to look. Our vision can be focused so tightly within the restrictions of our job or home, that we miss the vast world around us which is waiting to be seen and touched. We see a little and miss so much. One man concludes that a section of land is ugly and worthless. An artist glances at it and sees a hidden beauty which he seeks to transfer to his canvas. A student is ignored because no one sees any promise in him. But a teacher encourages him and watches as his potential is slowly fanned into life. A salesman resigns his territory because he sees the people as backward and country. Another views the same territory as an untapped region which is only waiting for a willing salesman. "Genius," William James once said, "means little more than the faculty of perceiving in an unhabitual way."[8]

Helen Keller, who was blind and deaf since she was eighteen months old, asked a friend of hers what she had seen after she returned from a walk in the woods. "Nothing in particular," her friend commented. Miss Keller noted that long ago she had observed that "the seeing see little." She then related what she had often "seen" in her walk in the woods. Through her touch alone, she felt the delicate symmetry of a leaf, the smooth skin of a silver birch, the rough, shaggy bark of a pine, the velvety texture of a flower, the cool waters of a brook, the lush carpet of pine needles, the quiver of a bird as she held a small tree, and so much more. All of these spoke to her about the panorama of nature and its wonders. To take our vision for granted is a terrible sin.[9] Miss Keller challenged us again:

> I who am blind can give one hint to those who see: use your eyes as if tomorrow you would be stricken blind. And the same method can be applied to the other senses. Hear the music of voices, the song of a bird, the mighty strings of an orchestra, as if you would be stricken deaf tomorrow. Touch each object you want to touch as if tomorrow your tactile sense would fail. Smell the perfume of flowers, taste with relish each morsel, as if tomorrow you could never smell and taste again. Make the most of every sense; glory in all the facets of pleasure and beauty.[10]

I know I fail to see so many things I used to see when I was a child. I do not take time to see the sky so blue anymore. The grass does not appear as green. I have little time to *see* the birds, or butterflies, glowworms, rocks, trees, or rivers. I sometimes pass through a crowd of people in an airport and see so few. Many faces fade into each other in the rush for the next plane. I sometimes do not really see the waitress who served me my meal in the restaurant. I did not seem to see some of my children's lives go by. It came so quickly, and I was so busy. I hardly noticed that I had grown older until the other day. Sometimes when I am deeply honest, I must confess that I have not always seen too clearly or too far. How about you? Be honest now. Have you always been able to see? I do not think I have been alone in my moments of blindness.

One day a man was walking with his grandson over the family farm. As they passed through the apple orchard, the grandfather said to the boy, "Jimmy, bring me an apple from one of the trees and break it open. What do you see in there?" "Some small seeds," the boy replies. "Break one of them open and then tell me what do you see?" "Nothing," Jimmy declared. "My boy," the grandfather observed, "where you see nothing, there a mighty apple tree dwells." Oh, for eyes to see beyond the known into the unknown, the familiar into the unfamiliar. We need eyes to see possibilities and freshness. We need eyes not dimmed with neglect or apathy. Oh, Lord, we cry, "Let us see again!"

Have you ever thought what eyes Jesus must have had? Jesus saw so much more than other men. While his disciples were awed by a giant Temple, Jesus saw a poor widow contributing sacrificially. Even in the midst of crowds, Jesus saw the needs of children, the helpless, the blind, or the sick. In the most ordinary things, He was able to perceive the splendor of the divine. A part of His ministry was to bring healing to the eyes of the blind. Could this not apply to the "seeing" blind? Jesus Christ saw as no man ever saw. In a common, ordinary fisherman He saw the writer of a Gospel. In a tax-collector and in the prostitute, Mary Magdalene, He saw faithful disciples. In a pharisaical heretic named Saul, He saw an apostle to the

Gentiles. "Blessed are the pure in heart, for they shall see." We shall see as we have never been able to see by walking in pilgrimage with the Christ. Only through His power can our vision be fully corrected.

Many feel that a person cannot change, that he or she cannot "see" differently. They cry, "An old dog cannot be taught new tricks," or "a leopard cannot change his spots." This is the conclusion that Eve reached in her conversation with Adam in George Bernard Shaw's play *Back to Methuselah*. Adam lamented that while he liked Eve, he did not like himself. He was tired of himself, desired to change, wanted to be different and better. The thought of spending forever in his present condition filled him with dread. Eve replied that she never worried about such things. She was what she was, and nothing could alter the situation.[11]

This is not the New Testament view of us; we *can* begin again. The possibility of "new birth," the place of "beginning again" is the "good news" of the Christian message. "Therefore, if any one is in Christ, he is a new creation; the old has passed away, behold, the new has come" (2 Cor. 5:17).

Learning to See God

There is a great longing within all persons to see God. Isaiah said that he "saw the Lord sitting upon a throne, high and lifted up" (Isa. 6:1). Moses declared that he saw the "goodness" of the Lord pass before him, although he was not permitted to see the "face" of God (Ex. 33:12-23). Paul affirmed that he saw a light brighter than the sun, and heard a voice out of the radiance calling him by name (Acts 26:12-18). From Patmos John said, "In the midst of the seven candlesticks I saw one like unto the Son of man" (Rev. 1:13, KJV). Passages like these reveal rich, vital encounters which certain individuals have had with God.

But they do not necessarily make us feel comfortable, because we know that we may never see God in that way.

In the court language of the ancient Hebrews, to see the king's face was something which was reserved for his favorite subjects. To be admitted into the king's presence was the desire of all subjects. It was the highest honor. Tennyson, who said that his greatest desire was a clear vision of God, requested that his poem, "Crossing the Bar," always be put at the end of his works. In it he expressed the deepest desire of many: "I hope to see my pilot face to face When I have crossed the bar."[12]

Many have longed to see God. But the same Scriptures which call persons to come to God, caution that it is impossible for them to see God. "There shall no man see me, and live," God declared to Moses (Ex. 33:20, KJV). Jesus also warned that "No man hath seen God at any time" (John 1:18, KJV). Some persons have had visions of God, but no one can literally see God with his or her physical sense. To see God, in the biblical sense, means to enter into His presence and friendship. It is to enter into such a vital communion with God, that our spiritual vision enables us to see, as Elizabeth Barrett Browning observed, that "Earth's crammed with heaven, And every common bush afire with God."[13] The Italian painter Raphael was once asked how he painted such beautiful pictures. "I simply dream dreams and see visions," he said, "and then I paint around those dreams and visions."

The pure in heart are able to see while others remain blind. Like Jesus, the pure in heart have learned to see God in the common, ordinary, and routine circumstances of life. Jesus told His disciples: "He that hath seen me hath seen the Father" (John 14:9, KJV). Not everyone who saw Jesus saw his Father through Him. Everyone does not see God through Him or through the world around them today, but those who have spiritual eyes to see, do. Paul affirmed that one day we shall see God fully. "Now we see through a glass, darkly; but then face to face: now I know in part; but then shall I know even as also I am known" (1 Cor. 13:12).

There is a Hebrew legend which says that when God created man and woman and breathed life into them, He gave them every treasure they needed but one. Satisfaction with this earthly life was withheld so that they would not be content with temporal and transient things but live with a longing, discontent, and restlessness which only eternity would satisfy. As Augustine once prayed: "Thou hast made us for thyself, O God, and restless are our souls until they rest in Thee. . . ."[14] As deep calls to deep, we learn to "see" God.

In his autobiography, *Eighty Adventurous Years*, Sherwood Eddy told how he was a selfish and cynical student at Yale until he went to hear the evangelist, Dwight L. Moody, preach. Reflecting on this experience, he noted:

> Before he had finished, I saw myself as I was—no good to my college, to my country, to man, or to God. I also saw Moody as he was, an uneducated man using bad grammar, but under God shaking the continent of America as he had moved the colleges and cities of Great Britain. A great thirst sprang up in my heart. Oh for a man to rise in me, that the man I was might cease to be! That night I forgot about my "good time." I went out into the field and by a great rock I wrestled with my own selfishness and sin. That night marked a turning point in my life. God became forever real to me.[15]

Can you remember when you first saw God and He was real to you? Maybe it was when you were a child, a teenager, or a young adult. But you can feel even now the sensation of life that surged within you as you yielded your life to God. Your outlook was different, your spirit firmer, your disposition brighter, your walk more vigorous, your hopes stronger, your drives more assuring, your goals more challenging, your attitude kinder, and your faith more vital. As the years have passed, has your faith waned, your assurance lessened, and your vision faded? Wordsworth's struggle is often our own:

It is not now as it hath been of yore:
Turn wheresoe'er I may,
By night or day,
The things which I have seen I now can see no more.[16]

Constantly we need to come into the presence of God through worship, prayer, and service that our vision can be reaffirmed, supported, nurtured, and sustained. One's relationship to God is not an encounter which is for a moment and then is over. It is a relationship that has a beginning and a point of contact for continuous growth and development. "But thanks be to God," Paul wrote, "that you who were once slaves of sin have become obedient from the heart to the standard of teaching to which you were committed, and, having been set free from sin, have become slaves of righteousness" (Rom. 6:17-18).

The blessedness of the pure in heart carries its own satisfaction. What greater joy can a person experience than to have his life so ordered and directed that he or she is able to sense the presence of God everywhere? Although the way is narrow and often like the eye of a needle, those who choose to follow the Master and become persons of the way have found the path that leads to the abundant life. In this Beatitude, however, there is a warning: It is only the pure in heart who will see God. The heart that is not made clean by the fellowship of the redeeming Christ cannot expect to be ushered into the presence of the Holy God.

Notes

1. Paul Scherer, *Facts that Undergird Life* (New York: Harper & Brothers, 1938), pp. 129-130.
2. Quoted in Gerald Kennedy, *With Singleness of Heart* (New York: Harper and Row, 1951), p. 15.
3. Ibid., p. 16.
4. Margaret Mitchell, *Gone with the Wind* (New York: Macmillan Publishing Co., Inc., 1936), pp. 710-711.
5. Robert Bolt, *A Man for All Seasons* (New York: Vintage Books, 1962), p. 81.
6. William F. Dean, "My Three Years as a Dead Man," *Saturday Evening Post* (February 13, 1954), p. 25.
7. Charles Schulz, *Peanuts*, United Feature Syndicate, Inc., Aug. 15, 1972.
8. William James, *The Principles of Psychology*. Vol. II (New York: Henry Holt & Co., 1896), p. 110.
9. Helen Keller, "Three Days to See," (Pawling, N.Y.: Foundation for Christian Living, n.d.), pp. 4-5.
10. Ibid., p. 12.
11. George Bernard Shaw, *Back to Methuselah* (New York: Dodd, Mead and Company, 1941), p. 4.
12. *The Poems of Alfred Lord Tennyson* (New York: Walter J. Black, Inc., 1922), p. 308.
13. Elizabeth Barrett Browning, *Aurora Leigh*, Book VII
14. *The Confessions of St. Augustine,* translated by E. P. Pusey (New York: E. P. Dutton Co., 1953), p. 1.
15. Sherwood Eddy, *Eighty Adventurous Years* (New York: Harper & Brothers, 1955), p. 27.
16. William Wordsworth, "Ode: Intimations of Immortality from Recollections of Early Childhood," in *English Romantic Poets* edited by James Stephens, et al (New York: American Book Co., 1952), p. 63.

"I have spoken these things to you that you might have peace in me." The opposite of this peace is scatteredness and chaos. Jesus speaks of the scattering, then of the bond with the Father, then of peace. Peace is what will overcome their desertion, what will bring them together again. Peace is their being back together in wholeness of relationship to him and to one another. His teaching points them to a peace grounded in his victory, a peace the essence of which is the corporate union with him. And to be in union with the Victor is to live out that victory.

—Dale Aukerman, *Darkening Valley: A Biblical Perspective on Nuclear War.*

7

Waging Peace

Blessed are the peacemakers, for they shall be called sons of God (Matt. 5:9).

My two children, who were then five and seven years old, were sitting on the floor one Saturday morning in January of 1973, watching the parade of cartoons. Suddenly the cartoons were interrupted as stately men gathered around a huge table to sign the Vietnam peace agreement. My young son looked up at me and asked, "Daddy, what is war?" I paused to look at innocence and childhood which did not yet know the pagan god, Mars. The wonders of it fascinated me. How grand it seemed to me to live in a world without the knowledge of war. But how quickly this dream has been shattered for so many through many centuries. In thirty-five-hundred years of recorded history, only one year in fifteen has not been spent in bloody wars. We are too familiar with "wars and rumors of wars," and so we need to acquaint ourselves again with the way of peace.

The War Trap

Trying to learn the way of peace in an age when men and women have lived and died in too many wars is like trying to sow grass seed in a hurricane. Seeds of peace have a difficult time growing in the soil of a thermonuclear age. All of our talk about peace is confronted by negations and contradictions. As a nation we talk about peace, but over $300 billion of our national budget is geared for military allotments. Since 1946 our nation's budget for military power has continued to increase rapidly while what we spend on education, health, labor and welfare programs, housing and community development continues to decline. We have a Defense Department but none for peace. We praise and decorate our men of war but seldom our men of peace.

Herman Kahn, a renowned weapons analyst, has written a book *Thinking About the Unthinkable* whose very title depicts the situation facing the world today. The awesome power of nuclear war is unthinkable with its "megacorpses," or millions dead. The missiles, antimissiles, Polaris-armed submarines, and other explosives in the United States and Soviet Union stockpiles alone, have explosive power equivalent to fifteen tons of TNT for every man, woman, and child in the world. Our world has moved into a war trap.

Civilization now has the potential for self-destruction with the awesome power of thermonuclear bombs. It is difficult to believe, but nevertheless true, that a single twenty-megaton H-bomb can deliver "more explosive power than that of all the weapons used by all nations for all purposes during all the years of World War II."[1]

Our nation has recently launched the largest peacetime military buildup in its history. The nuclear arms race has escalated from only two nuclear weapons in 1945 to over fifty thousand in 1981. This includes nine-thousand strategic nuclear bombs and another twenty-two-thousand tactical nuclear bombs which the United States possesses. While the Soviets have approximately six-thousand strategic and fifteen-thousand tactical bombs.[2] The possibility of a nuclear war is real and frightening. Several other countries already have nuclear weapons, and it is predicted that by 1990 thirty-five other nations may have them. The horrendous destructive power of these weapons today is rarely appreciated. Each of our Poseidon submarines has ten missiles, and each of these carries fourteen MIRV warheads. This means, as John R. W. Stott has alerted us, that each submarine has enough destructive force to destroy 140 Hiroshimas. The nuclear warheads which the United States has "could annihilate the complete world population 12 times over."[3] There exists today destructive power beyond prediction. "War, now nuclear war," Dale Aukerman declared, "is the key issue not only for survival but also for coming to grips before God with who we are."[4]

With the threat of this unprecedented danger, it would seem that a nuclear war could not even be an option. However, wars are seldom begun as the result of logic or rational judgment. Nuclear war might result from miscalculation, accidents, escalation, conquest for power, irresponsibility, or some aggressive military action. "There can scarcely be any real victory over the enemy in an atomic war," Albert Schweitzer observed. "Neither of the two major opponents is significantly superior to the other. The defeated side can inflict such terrible damage upon the victor that victory will be meaningless!"[5]

Humanity has often wrapped itself in a military security blanket. Peace is not achieved at the threat of instant annihilation. Reconciliation, not destruction, is the path to Christian peace. "The question," Senator Mark Hatfield has observed, "is not whether we should have an army, but rather, whether our trust rests solely in our military power as a means of insuring our security and peace. The Scripture does not condone such a trust."[6] Arnold Toynbee wrote in his momentous work *A Study of History* that "warfare is the commonest cause of breakdown of civilization during the four or five millennia."[7] "Violence in our world is interconnected. It is chain reactive," Norman

Cousins has noted. "It runs from the small to the large and back again, from the half-crazed individual with a handgun to space armadas with explosives that can incinerate whole cities, from men who have contempt for law to nations that refuse to consider the establishment of law in the world."[8]

War is violence on its most destructive level. Robert E. Lee was probably correct when he said, "It is well that war is so terrible, or we should grow too fond of it."[9] "The importance of securing international peace was recognized by the really great men of former generations," noted the great physicist, Albert Einstein. But the technical advances of our times have turned this ethical postulate into a matter of life and death for civilized mankind today, and made the taking of an active part in the solution of the problem of peace a moral duty which no conscientious man can shirk.[10]

The world-famous evangelist Billy Graham spoke out against the terrifying arms race and the need for nations to face their own hour of decision about halting the escalation of nuclear weapons. "I honestly wish we had never developed nuclear weapons, . . . " Graham said, "I believe that the Christian especially has a responsibility to work for peace in our world."[11]

In the closing years of his life, Schweitzer gave much of his energy to the problem of atomic war and attempted to challenge us to find a spiritual and ethical solution rather than a military and political one. The possibility of another war to him was seen as an unmitigated catastrophe and he called for nations to settle their differences by peaceful negotiations. "A new kind of patriotism," he said, "must arise; the new patriot must be able to feel more humanly and see farther than patriots of the past."[12]

Men and women need to arise in our generation who really believe in the peace of God and who will identify themselves with the spiritual goals and purposes of God. Men and women are needed who believe in the kingdom of God and who will not only pray that it will come but who will dedicate themselves to that end. "As we, if we are to find peace, must have faith in the spiritual future of our own nation, so too must we have faith in the spiritual future of all mankind," said Schweitzer in a sermon preached on October 13, 1918, after returning from an internment camp of St. Remy de Provence. "Some progress must come; a race of men must arise to form nations united by spiritual goals, attempting the highest that can be achieved on earth."[13]

Charles Schulz, the cartoonist of *Peanuts*, in his intriguing way reflected this problem in one of his features. Linus and Charlie Brown were talking to another boy, who was holding a toy rifle in his hand. Linus was speaking: "A wooden rifle with a rubber bayonet! Boy, is that ever slick! Gee I wish I had one of those. . . . I'm always intrigued by educational toys!"[14] Out of the mouths of babes come insights about modern man's own notions of education and power.

A small step has been taken in this direction. In November, 1978, President Carter signed legislation creating the Commission on Proposals for the National Academy of Peace and Conflict Resolution. Congress appropriated half-a-million dollars for this commission, which is according to Colman McCarthy, "the equivalent of about two minutes of the Defense Department budget." This academy would seek to school persons for peace. One of the big persons behind this effort is Milton Mapes. He envisions that graduates from this academy would serve, hopefully, in positions in government, the Foreign Service, the armed forces, corporations, labor unions, private organizations, and in many other places. They would strive to create alternatives to violence in our world.[15]

During the Second World War, Harry Emerson Fosdick preached a sermon in which he cautioned Americans against "worshiping the gods of a beaten enemy."[16] The Book of 2 Chronicles relates the story of how Judah won a war against the Edomites, and when Amaziah, the Judean king, came back in triumph to Jerusalem, he brought the gods of the children of Edom and bowed down and worshiped before them. Having fought so many wars, we are now beginning to believe that the only way to peace is by military power. Humanity is now bowing at the altar of Mars, the god of war. Is the road to peace found by copying our enemies and adopting their ways? At the close of the Second World War, someone observed: "If we are wise, we will never allow ourselves to go down into the pit of hell and come up expecting our spirits to be redeemed." We must escape the war-trap mentality if we are to tread the way of peace.

Peace Within Ourselves

"So many forces are pulling at me," the young woman said, "that I feel I am going to fly all to pieces. My husband wants this, my children demand something else, my parents want me to be more attentive to them, my children's school, my clubs, my church, all want so much of me. How can I keep my sanity?" Life does seem to pull at us at times, and it pulls like wild horses straining in opposite directions, as though we would be ripped apart. Few of us have learned to live with the tension of affirming self and denying self, of knowing that "I am OK" yet "not OK." Each of us reaches to affirm who and what he or she is *not* as well as who and what he or she *is.* On occasions we feel that Carl Sandburg is correct; we have "a menagerie within us."[17]

The tempo of today's world has caused many to become sick, fatigued, confused, misguided, frustrated, irritated, exasperated, defeated, disappointed, or disconcerted. J. B. Phillips, in noting the complexity and speed of modern living, has stated, "Inward peace is not merely the absence of outward worry and strain. What we need is a positive peace which will keep us calm and poised, even when outward things are dark and difficult. Here the Christian faith offers us a *gift.*"[18] The gift is Christ's peace (John 14:27; Phil. 4:7).

Before there can be peace in the world, persons must end the civil war raging within themselves, bring their own life in harmony with God, and restore their fractured relationship to others. The Chinese have a proverb that the longest journey begins with the first step. The Christian peacemaker must begin first with himself or herself. Thirty years ago Rabbi Joshua Liebman pleaded for inward tranquility as the essential ingredient for a meaningful life. "I have come to understand that peace of mind," he wrote, "is the characteristic mark of God himself, and that it has always been the true goal of the considered life."[19] His book *Peace of Mind* launched a new movement within our country. Although some voices within this movement have almost reduced the Christian faith to a sort of "peace of mind" philosophy, there is no question that inner peace is a basic characteristic of genuine Christian faith. The popularity of the writings of this movement also attests to a deep need within men and women for an inner calm.

In the announcement of the birth of Jesus the angel said, "Glory to God in the highest, and on earth peace, good will toward men" (Luke 2:14, KJV). On the eve of His death, aware of His impending death, surrounded by fearful disciples, Jesus offered a peace to His disciples which was evidence of His own security. "Peace I leave with you, my peace I give unto you: not as the world giveth, give I unto you. Let not your heart be troubled, neither let it be afraid" (John 14:27, KJV). His bequest came from His own inner calmness and stability.

Sometimes it is difficult for us to understand how one could have such peace in the midst of such turbulent conditions as Jesus faced. The word for *peace* in the Bible, however, is not only a negative word for the absence of trouble or difficulty but a positive word which conveys the idea of right relationships, intimacy, and everything that makes life worth living in its highest sense. Peace is an inner stability which is not conditioned or determined by external circumstances. According to the Bible, this kind of peace has its rootage in God Himself. "Grace be to you, and peace, from God our Father, and from the Lord Jesus Christ" (Eph. 1:2, KJV). "In quietness and in confidence shall be your strength" (Isa. 30:15, KJV). "In peace I will both lie down and sleep; for thou alone, O Lord, makest me dwell in safety" (Ps. 4:8).

The word *peace* was often on the lips of the early Christians. Jesus frequently said, "Go in peace," or "Peace be with you" (Mark 5:34; John 20:19). At the beginning and conclusion of many New Testament letters, Paul and others sent greetings of peace (Gal. 1:3; Eph. 1:2; 1 Pet. 1:2; Jude 2). The peace which Christ offers to us enables us to understand who we are, to love ourselves, and to accept ourselves as we have been accepted already through the love of God. His peace overcomes our split nature and brings us wholeness within. For the Christian, peace or inner serenity is received as a gift from Christ (John 14:-27); it is one of the fruits of the spirit (Gal. 5:22); and Paul declared that "the peace of God, which passeth all understanding, shall keep your hearts and minds through Christ Jesus" (Phil 4:7, KJV). "Keep the boat steady," Jim Hawkins is told in Robert Louis Stevenson's novel, *Treasure Island.* "How can I keep it steady," responds the boy, "when I'm not steady inside?" Real peace comes from being constant and unwavering within by the inner presence of the Spirit of Christ.

The peace which Jesus offers us does not exempt us from all pain, suffering, problems, and difficulties. Many faithful Christians have experienced years of agony, pain, and trouble. The peace which Jesus offers us is not a magical escape from all hardships and troubles. According to Luke 21:8-19, Jesus said that the Christian might suffer wars, physical calamities, economic loss, and many other distresses. God "spared not his own Son, but delivered him up for us all" (Rom. 8:32, KJV). The Prince of Peace Himself was met by rejection, hostility, denial, torture, and cruel death. His peace was achieved not by separation from the troubles and agony of mankind, but rather was an inward calm which He experienced in the midst of the "storms" around Him.

For several years my family and I lived in Slidell, Louisiana, a small town, across Lake Pontchartrain from New Orleans. While we were living there the area was struck by several devastating hurricanes with winds in excess of 120 miles an hour. I shall never forget the howling winds which shook our house as though a giant force had its grip on it, and the pounding rain which beat down upon the house like watery hammers with a ceaseless rhythm, and the awful feeling within of whether or not the house could continue to withstand such pressures upon it. Then, suddenly and unexpectedly, although I had read about it, and heard about it, a great calm engulfed the area, and the storm ceased. The sun came out, the birds began to sing again, and all seemed peaceful and quiet. Here, to my amazement, was the calm at the center of the hurricane. Later the other side of the hurricane hit with all of its force, and I was keenly aware that the storm was not yet over.

The lesson, however, of the tranquility and peacefulness in the eye of a ravaging hurricane remains with me to this day. It is for me a parable about the inner peace which Jesus gives to us. "Peace I leave with you; my peace I give to you; not as the world gives do I give to you. Let not your hearts be troubled," Jesus said to His disciples, "neither let them be afraid" (John 14:27-28). The peace which Jesus gives to His followers does not remove us from the storms, but it is a calmness at the center of our being. It is a "peace which passes all understanding" (Phil. 4:7).

The inner peace we seek has been pictured by Charles Morgan as "the stilling of the soul within the activities of the mind and body so that it might be still as the axis of a revolving wheel is still." The inner calmness which Christ offers to us is in the midst of our activities, labors, struggles, and responsibilities, and not isolated from them.

Inner peace teaches us many valuable lessons which enable us to face life and its struggles. This kind of peace gives us a new perspective. "Peace is the assurance that failure is not so much our enemy as our teacher. Peace is the awareness that pain is not so much our enemy," Myron and Mary Madden wrote, "as our opportunity to learn. Peace is knowing that there are loving, helping hearts that can alert us and are willing to share our stress."[20] This kind of peace arms us to live in the midst of trouble and change. This peace affords a calm which does not flee from all difficulties and uncertainties.

Paul had found this inner peace in the grace and love of God, and He was convinced that nothing could separate Him from this strength. "Who shall separate us from the love of Christ?" he asked. He continued by affirming:

> Shall tribulation, or distress, or persecution, or famine, or nakedness, or peril, or sword? . . . No, in all these things

we are more than conquerors through him who loved us. For I am sure that neither death, nor life, nor angels, nor principalities, nor things present, nor things to come, nor powers, nor height, nor depth, nor anything else in all creation, will be able to separate us from the love of God in Christ Jesus our lord (Rom. 8:35; 37-39).

Peaceful Relationships

Peace is not merely a quality which a person keeps hidden down inside himself. A peaceful person is one who seeks to establish right relationships between people. Society is filled with quarreling, bitterness, conflicts, and disagreements. The Christian is not just a lover of peace, but he or she is a peacemaker. Our responsibility is to help persons become reconciled to each other. The peacemakers are those who are trying to remove the cause of strife that separates persons. Divisions and splits have given us a disjointed world. The Berlin Wall, the Iron Curtain, the Bamboo Curtain, lines of demarcation, class against class, race against race, the generation gap, white-collar against blue-collar workers, hard hats against the dissenters, and more reveal our estrangement from each other.

Where does healing begin? Our discord is not concerned alone with war and international problems. To be peacemakers, we must begin where we are. The deacon who asserts that he is the one in his church that always kept things from being unanimous is not a peacemaker yet. The woman who declares that she will never be the one to say she is sorry has a distance to travel before becoming a peacemaker. The church member who states that "those kind of folks" are not good enough for our church is not yet a reconciler. The neighbor who says that "he doesn't care about what might be better for his community, his only concern is with his own piece of private property" has not learned the difference between isolation and peace. A woman who was having difficulty getting along with a neighbor from another country who is now living here avowed: "If I cannot get along with one person from another country, what hope is there for better international relations?" We must begin where we are with our neighbors and friends. One of the characters in the novel, *The Brothers Karamazov*, by Dostoevski has indicated the problems with which many of us live: "The more I love humanity in general, the less I love man in particular."21

Harry and Bonaro Overstreet have observed that individuals who remake hostile situations into ones of mutual good will are creative artists. Drawing from Browning's *Abt Vogler*, they give an image of an artist like a great musical composer who is able "out of three sounds" to frame "not a fourth sound, but a star." "The composer, in short," they note, "makes new unity out of already existing elements; and this is precisely what the genuine peacemaker does." Continuing with this image they concluded:

> He does not try to make his opponent over in his own image. His concern is to make the situation that includes both himself and his opponent into one where human powers and individual traits that have not been called forth by conflict will be called forth and made the basis of shared rather than antagonistic action.

> The sounds with which the musical composer works are neither new nor peculiarly his. As Browning reminds us, they are "everywhere in the world. . . . " He does not need better sounds: the old ones will become a new magic if he is able so to feel their intrinsic qualities that he can bring them together into a new mutually supporting unity.22

In the New Testament Jesus Christ is called *Mediator*. This title, when applied to Jesus, means more than someone between God and mankind, Frank Stagg declared. "Jesus came *to overcome the betweenness* between God and man."[23] In Jesus Christ we have experienced reconciliation with God and from Him we have now received a ministry of reconciliation. "And all things are of God, who hath reconciled us to himself by Jesus Christ, and hath given to us the ministry of reconciliation" (2 Cor. 5:18, KJV). We are now to help "overcome the betweenness" between persons.

During our nation's terrible Civil War, the famous Southern general, Robert E. Lee, was severely criticized by one of his fellow officers, General Whiting. On one occasion Jefferson Davis, the president of the Confederacy, summoned General Lee in for consultation and asked his opinion of General Whiting. Lee commended Whiting as an able officer and soldier. There was present in the room at the same time another officer who pulled Lee aside and asked if he were aware of the unkind criticisms which Whiting had voiced against him. Lee indicated that he was aware of the criticisms, but he stated that he understood that President Davis wanted to know what he thought of Whiting and not what Whiting thought of him.

This kind of magnanimous spirit is the pathway to living as a peacemaker. It is not an easy way, nevertheless it is the way of not only a noble spirit but the Christlike path itself. "He that would love life and see good days, let him keep his tongue from evil and his lips from speaking guile; let him turn away from evil and do right; let him seek peace and pursue it" (1 Pet. 3:10-11).

Wage Peace

How do we achieve peace? Does it come about by someone saying "Let's have some peace and quiet around here"? Then everyone immediately complies. Is it realized by responding affirmatively to the policeman who declares, "Listen boys, we don't want no trouble here"? Peace, in the biblical sense, means much more than the absence of trouble or the cessation of strife and conflict. It is not something which will be realized by merely thinking or studying about it. Jesus did not say, "Blessed are those who study about peace, pray for peace, love peace, or even desire peace." He said, "Blessed are the peacemakers." We need to want peace, to study about it, love it, and pray for it, but, above all, we must work for it. Just as war is waged; so peace must be waged. Peace requires effort, initiative, sacrifice, devotion, and commitment.

"We have had our last chance. If we do not now devise some greater and more equitable system, Armageddon will be at our door," General MacArthur declared at the surrender of Japan. "The problem basically is theological and involves a spiritual recrudescence and improvement of human character. . . . It must be of the spirit if we are to save the flesh."[24] The church has the great responsibility of waging peace in the world today. If the church does not assume the leadership role in being peacemakers, who else can be expected to take up this assignment? The poet, John Milton, reminded us that "Peace hath her victories / No less renowned than war."[25] "We have tried war and it is found wanting," exclaimed Frank Stagg. "We must find an alternative to war. If Christians worked as hard to eliminate war as many have to justify it, it could make a difference."[26] It is the goal of the peacemaker to lead our world to turn its efforts toward peace and not war.

Think of the difference in the world if our scientific and medical research could be directed to peaceful pursuits. Imagine the modifications we could have in our world if the factories and plants hummed for peaceful ends; consider the revolution which could take place in our world if the politicians worked endlessly for peace; dream of the innovations which could be produced in our world if the efforts put toward military purposes could be channeled for peace instead of war. Would we, then, have arrived at the place where the wolf and the lamb could lie down together as Isaiah envisioned (Isa. 11:6-7)? When will the time come that nations "shall beat their swords into plowshares, and their spears into pruning hooks; nation shall not lift up sword against nation, neither shall they learn war any more" (Isa. 2:4)? As peacemakers, we not only long for this day but work for it that men and women and nations shall believe and practice the teaching that "The wisdom from above is first pure, then peaceable, gentle, open to reason, full of mercy and good fruits, without uncertainty or insincerity. And the harvest of righteousness is sown in peace by those who make peace" (Jas. 3:17-18).

No one expects a flower garden to remain beautiful if the weeds are pulled up in the early spring and then it is left alone for the rest of the summer. Flower gardens require constant weeding. War must be waged against the weeds. Peace cannot survive in a world crowding it out with weeds of hatred, hostility, mistrust, ignorance, misunderstandings, prejudice, violence, oppression, and war. Peace must be the hoe to remove the forces that curtail its growth. Or to change the metaphor, the Christian needs to be the scalpel which seeks to cut out whatever obstructs peace. As Francis of Assisi prayed, "Lord, make me an instrument of thy peace. . . ." As instruments and peacemakers for God in the world, we have been given our marching orders. The challenge is to be, do, and go—not to sit, rest, and recline.

Often church assemblies or conventions pass resolutions against war and proclaim that "war is incompatible with the life and teachings of Jesus Christ." That, of course, is true. But it no more deals with the real issue than a medical convention voting that "cancer is incompatible with the health of persons" can bring about a cure for cancer. A cure can come only when the cause of the problem is countered. Cancerous disease is removed, if possible. Peacemakers work to remove the "disease" within persons which keeps them from being reconciled with God, self, and others. Resolutions are not the answer. Peace must be waged.

Sometimes we need to ask ourselves whether we really love peace or whether we only hate war. Loving or waging peace means being willing to work at improving relationships, bridging gaps of misunderstandings, listening without preconceived judgments, correcting rumors, making some concessions or compromises, searching for truth and not just opinions, forgiving errors or mistakes, supporting rather than destroying those weaker than we are, and surrendering some of our own desires when it is for the common good. To wage peace our feet must be shod "with the equipment of the gospel of peace" (Eph. 6:15).

We look for strength to wage the peacelike way in the name of the one whom Isaiah proclaimed as the "Wonderful Counselor, Mighty God, Everlasting Father, Price of Peace" (Isa. 9:6). We long for the realization of the lyric commendation from Isaiah centuries ago. "How beautiful upon the mountains are the feet of him who brings good tidings, who publishes peace" (52:7).

The peacemaker follows the Prince of Peace and takes the initiative to overcome hostility. In small quarrels the peacemaker is willing to make the first step. In national and global problems, he seeks to lend his support to fight for truth and justice even at the risk of misunderstanding or sometimes even rejection.

In a Christmas issue of *Home Missions* magazine, the

editor, Walker Knight, devoted the issue to "The Peace-maker." Here is a brief portion from this beautiful prose-poetry article about peace.

> It's not just hating war, despising war,
>   sitting back and waiting for war to end.
> It's not just loving peace, wanting peace,
>   sitting back and waiting for peace to come,
> Peace, like war, is waged.
> Peace plans its strategy and encircles the enemy.
> Peace marshals its forces and storms the gates.
> Peace gathers its weapons and pierces the defense.
> The weapons of peace are love, joy, goodness,
>   long-suffering.
> The arms of peace are truth, honesty, patience, prayer.
> The strategy of peace brings safety, welfare, happiness.
> The forces of peace are the sons of God.
>
> Now Christ has turned it around!
> I am to love my enemy.
> . . . do good to those who hate me.
> . . . turn the other cheek.
> I am salt, so I attack to save.
> I am leaven, so I penetrate to quicken.
> I am light, so I shine to illumine.
>
> I serve the Prince of Peace
> His ever-expanding, peaceful government will never
>   end.
> He will rule with perfect fairness and justice
>   from the throne of his father David.
> He will bring true justice and peace
>   to all the nations of the world.
>
> He has made me a Peacemaker,
>   and he has given me the ministry of
>   reconciliation.[27]

In Albert Camus' disturbing novel, *The Plague,* a port town, Oran, on the Algerian coast, was shut off from the rest of the world as the Black Death moved in its haunted, ghoulish agony across the city, leaving behind its anguish of cruelty, pain, grief, and countless victims. Dr. Rieux, the town's physician, observed the outward and inward responses of the plague-stricken people and concluded that "there are more things to admire in men than to despise." Aware that the battle against the plague was a never-ending conflict, Dr. Rieux looked at the joyous crowd after the quarantine had been lifted and realized that "joy is always imperiled." "He knew that those jubilant crowds did not know but could have learned from books: that the plague bacillus never dies or disappears for good; that it can lie dormant for years and years in furniture and linen chests; that it bides its time in bedrooms, cellars, trunks, and bookshelves; and that perhaps the day would come when, for the bane and the enlightening of men, it would rouse up its rats again and send them forth to die in a happy city."[28]

Like the never-ending battle against infectious disease, there is a continuous struggle to bring peace in the world. It will not come easily nor quickly. Peace will have to be waged ceaselessly. War may lift its ugly head first in one country and then in another. The battle of waging peace has not yet been won. The church's responsibility is to give guidance and direction, men and women, voices and languages, equipment and supplies to wage the way of peace. May our prayer for all persons be that "The Lord bless you and keep you: The Lord make his face to shine upon you, and be gracious to you: The Lord lift up his countenance upon you, and give you peace" (Num. 6:24-26).

"Blessed are the peacemakers, for they shall be called sons of God." The Hebrew language is not strong in adjectives, and when it describes something it often uses the phrase "son of" and an abstract noun. A man, then, would not be called a peaceful man but a son of peace. Often we say, "That child is certainly like his father." To be a peacemaker is to be Godlike, because we are sharing in His work. God's ministry is reconciliation, and His sons and daughters, His children, share in this work. The blessedness of the peacemaker is to be engaged in the work of God as a child in His own family.

Notes

1. David Rittenhouse Inglis, "The Nature of Nuclear War," in *Nuclear Weapons and the Conflict of Conscience*, John C. Bennett, ed. (New York: Charles Scribner's Sons, 1962), p. 43.

2. Robert C. Aldridge, "The Deadly Race," *A Matter of Faith* (Washington, D.C., published by Sojourners, 1981), pp. 9-13.

3. John R. W. Stott, "Calling for Peacemaking in a Nuclear Age, Part I" *Christianity Today*, February 8, 1980.

4. Dale Aukerman, *Darkening Valley: A Biblical Perspective on Nuclear War* (New York: The Seabury Press, 1981), p. xvi.

5. Albert Schweitzer, *The Teachings of Reverence for Life* (New York: Holt, Rinehart, and Winston, 1965), p. 61.

6. Mark O. Hatfield, *Conflict and Conscience* (Waco, Tex.: Word Books, 1971), p. 48.

7. Arnold Toynbee, *A Study of History*, vol. 3 (London: Oxford University Press, 1934), p. 150.

8. Norman Cousins quoted by Ovid Demanis, *American the Violent* (New York: Cowles Book Company, Inc., 1970), pp. 381-382.

9. Carl Sandburg, *Abraham Lincoln: The War Years* (New York: Harcourt, Brace & Co., 1939), vol. I, p. 526.

10. Albert Einstein, *The World as I See It*, translated by Alan Harris (New York: Philosophical Library, 1949), p. 43.

11. "A Change of Heart: Billy Graham on the Nuclear Arms Race," *Sojourners* (August 1979).

12. Schweitzer, p. 53.

13. Albert Schweitzer, *Reverence for Life* (New York: Harper & Row, 1969), pp. 98-99.

14. Charles Schulz, *Peanuts*, United Feature Syndicate, 1958.

15. "A National Peace Academy: Promoting and Preserving Perpetual Peace" *Report from the Capitol* (February 1982), p. 7. Anyone interested in this effort may write the National Peace Institute Foundation, 110 Maryland Ave. N.E., Washington, D.C. 20002. For a good discussion and group guide, see Glen

Stassen, *The Journey into Peacemaking* (Memphis, TN: Brotherhood Commission of the SBC, 1983).

16. Harry Emerson Fosdick, *A Great Time to Be Alive* (New York: Harper & Brothers, 1944), p. 155*f.*

17. "Wilderness," *Complete Poems of Carl Sandburg* (New York: Harcourt, Brace and Co., 1950), pp. 100-101.

18. J. B. Phillips, *Is God at Home?* (Nashville: Abingdon Press, 1957), p. 102.

19. Joshua Loth Liebman, *Peace of Mind* (New York: Simon and Schuster, 1946), p. 4.

20. Myron C. and Mary Ben Madden, *The Time of Your Life* (Nashville: Broadman Press, 1977), p. 93.

21. Fedor Dostoevski, *The Brothers Karamazov* (Garden City, N.Y.: International Collectors Library, n.d.), p. 49.

22. Harry and Bonaro Overstreet, *The Mind Alive* (New York: W. W. Norton & Co., Inc., 1954), pp. 254-255.

23. Frank Stagg, *New Testament Theology* (Nashville: Broadman Press, 1962, p. 73.

24. Frazier Hunt, *The Untold Story of Douglas MacArthur* (New York: The Devin-Adain Company, 1954), p. 405.

25. John Milton, "To the Lord General Cromwell" *English Literature: A Period Anthology.* Edited by Albert C. Baugh and George McClelland. (New York: Appleton-Century-Crofts, Inc., 1954), p. 406.

26. Personal conversation with the writer.

27. Walker Knight, "The Peacemaker," *Home Missions* (Atlanta: Home Mission Board, Dec., 1972), p. 21.

28. Albert Camus, *The Plague* (New York: Vintage Books, 1972), p. 278.

I am not ashamed of the gospel of Christ in its insistence on the prodigious lifting power of vicarious sacrifice. Vicarious sacrifice is the most impressive fact in the moral world. What one of us has not been saved from something because another, who did not need to do it, voluntarly took on himself our calamity or sin and by self-sacrifice redeemed us? And wherever that spirit of the cross appears and the ancient words come alive again, "He saved others; himself he cannot save," there is the most subduing, humbling, impressive fact we see. How can a man be ashamed of that?

—Harry Emerson Fosdick, *Successful Christian Living.*

8

Standing to be Counted

Blessed are those who are persecuted for righteousness'
sake, for theirs is the kingdom of heaven. (Matt. 5:10).

Just as the speaker began a young man jumped up in the
congregation and began to shout: "You don't mean a word
of it! You sang, 'All to Jesus I surrender.' 'Where he leads
me I will follow.' 'Jesus, I my cross have taken.' How many
of us have done or would really do that?" The audience
sat stunned and unresponsive. It was a preplanned act on
the part of a group of young people at their annual fall
student convention. But its impact was felt by everyone
there. The question lingers even now in my mind, "Do we
really mean that we will follow Jesus anywhere, even into
persecution or death?" In the last Beatitude Jesus turns to
a strange dimension of "happiness," the bliss of those who
are persecuted for the sake of righteousness.

The Cost of Discipleship

When Jesus issued His invitation for men and women to
become His disciples, He did not drape his call in velvet
softness or tranquil bliss. He revealed the "sharp flint" at
the beginning. He was completely honest with those who
chose to follow Him. Instead of comfort, security, ease,
painless or effortless living, Jesus spoke candidly of self-
denial, taking up one's cross, forsaking all to follow Him,
turning the other cheek, going the second mile, and being

faithful unto death. To follow Christ was no promise of a bed of roses.

Charles Kettering, a leading American research scientist in the automotive industry, was asked once what the primary qualification of a research scientist is. "He must not bruise easily," he responded. These words are also very appropriate for a follower of Jesus Christ. The way of Christ will often be forbidding, harsh, and rigorous.

From the start Jesus indicated that His way might be difficult or hard. The first seven Beatitudes list the great Christian qualities which followers of Jesus should have. This Beatitude affirms the costly nature of trying to put these qualities into daily practice. It is not easy but costly. Later in the Sermon on the Mount Jesus confirmed His message on the nature of Christian discipleship as His followers are challenged to be the "salt," the "leaven," and "light" in the world. Having heard His teaching, His disciples are now to live by them. Living by them does not always bring acceptance or appreciation, but often rejection, hatred, hostility, and persecution.

Jesus did not say that every persecution is blessed. This happiness is promised only to those who are persecuted "for righteousness sake." If we are not liked by our neighbors, or cannot get along well with our family or business associates, this is not necessarily suffering for the sake of righteousness. It may be because we are self-righteous, austere, fastidious, intolerant, or dictatorial. The motive must be right to experience the happiness which Jesus is describing. But Jesus did expect His followers to be persecuted and He warned them what to expect. He pointed out clearly that His gospel has a sandpaper edge to it which will be offensive to many. Later He repeated His warnings to His disciples and told them to expect sacrifice, trouble, persecution, suffering, and even death.

But take heed to yourselves; for they will deliver you up to councils; and you will be beaten in synagogues; and you will stand before governors and kings for my sake, to bear testimony before them. And the gospel must first be preached to all nations. And when they bring you to trial and deliver you up, do not be anxious. . . . . And brother will deliver up brother to death, and the father his child, and children will rise against parents, and have them put to death; and you will be hated by all for my name's sake. But he who endures to the end will be saved (Mark 13:9-13).

See also John 15:18-19; Matt. 10:16-22; 1 Pet. 3:14). In His call to discipleship, Jesus revealed the demand it entails. "If any man will come after me, let him deny himself, and take up his cross and follow me. For whosoever will save his life shall lose it: and whosoever will lose his life for my sake shall find it" (Matt. 16:24-25, KJV).

Self-denial is never easy. One of the great all-time figures of a sacrificial spirit was Anne Sullivan Macy. One day she reached out to help a small seven-year-old child who was shut out by closed doors of blindness, deafness, and muteness. Mrs. Macy, who had known herself something of the experience of partial blindness, touched the life of Helen Keller, and it was never the same again. She poured her life vicariously into this small child and after much struggle opened up a new world to Keller. Later Miss Keller passed her college entrance exams, and later still graduated from college *cum laude*. Years later she became a world figure and was honored around the world. Harry Emerson Fosdick, who was Mrs. Macy's pastor, spoke of her powerful contribution to Miss Keller.

Still in the background was this magician, this self-effacing teacher, putting her life into another's and liberating it. It is one of the most amazing stories in the human record. And so powerful is such sacrifice that, because of this example of what can be done, new hopes have come, new methods, new open doors for blind and deaf folks everywhere, and the story has no end. Once more vicarious sacrifice works its miracle.[1]

The Faithful Witnesses

The Christian is above all a witness to what he or she has experienced in Jesus Christ. Gabriel Marcel, a French playright and philosopher, has stated that if a person is asked to be a witness in a legal matter, he is being called because he has some evidence concerning the case. "He must share what he knows, or he may bring harm to another human being. In bearing witness, a person commits himself by taking an oath and stakes his very fidelity on what he has seen or heard."[2] Christian witness is founded on personal religious experience, and our testimony grows out of that vital relationship. It is out of the roots of personal witness that the New Testament witness first arose.

> That which was from the beginning, which we have heard, which we have seen with our eyes, which we have looked upon and touched with our hands, concerning the word of life—the life was made manifest, and we saw it, and testify to it, and proclaim to you the eternal life which was with the Father and was made manifest to us—that which we have seen and heard we proclaim also to you, so that you may have fellowship with us; and our fellowship is with the Father and with his Son Jesus Christ (1 John 1:1-3).

Before the end of the first century the Greek words for *witness* and *martyr* had become synonymous. In the early days of the Christian faith, to be a faithful witness for Christ often meant that one would have to die for Him. Jesus Himself embodied the teachings of His Beatitudes. He was persecuted for righteousness sake and was eventually nailed to a cross. According to tradition, all of His twelve disciples, except one, John, met a violent death in their service for Christ. Before he was converted Paul had shared in the "threatenings and slaughter" against the early Christians. To follow Jesus Christ in the first century inevitably led to suffering and persecution. Why? Because to follow Jesus Christ was a call to be different and not be a part of the status quo.

Any person who seeks to live his or her life by the high moral standards of Jesus Christ in all relationships is often resented and hated by some. The early Christians, by their faithfulness to Jesus Christ, sometimes brought disruption into their home, their work, and their social life as they tried to be loyal to Christ. Slander and insults were often directed against the early Christians. They were accused of being atheists because they did not use images in their worship. Misunderstandings about the practice of the Lord's Supper led to accusations of cannibalism. The secrecy of their meetings and the celebration of the "Love Feast" led many to accuse them of immorality.

Politically the early Christians encountered persecution because of their refusal to participate in the various forms of Caesar worship. To the Romans the refusal of the Christians to acknowledge Caesar as Lord was not so much a religious act as a sign of political disloyalty. Religion to Rome was primarily a matter of patriotism. Rome saw the Christians as traitors to the state and potential revolutionaries, and, therefore, moved against them to keep what they feared might be another group from causing an uprising in the empire. The Christians were seen as a threat to the state.

From the time of the reign of Nero, the Christians were persecuted for nearly three-hundred years. Persecution under emperors Decius, Diocletian, and others was severe until the Edict of Milan in 313 established Christianity as the official religion of the Roman Empire. But throughout history, Christians have lived with various forms of persecution. Individuals like Polycarp of Smyrna, Justin Martyr, William Tyndale, Joan of Arc, and Tom Dooley were "faithful unto death." In the Middle Ages the Roman Catholic Church established the Inquisition to control heresy. Various confessional groups have persecuted others, some by physical violence and some by other means.

When John Hus attempted to reform the church in Bohemia, he encountered strong opposition from the ecclesiastical authorities. At the Council of Constance, he was judged by Cardinal d'Ailly and other accusers and was condemned as a heretic. On July 6, 1415, he was chained to a stake and burned. His persecutors put on his head a crown made of paper with painted devils on it. When Hus saw it, he declared, "My Lord Jesus Christ for my sake wore a crown of thorns. Why should not I, then, for his sake, wear this like crown, be it ever so ignominious? Truly I will do it, and that willingly." As the bishop sat the paper crown on the head of Hus, he said: "Now we commit thy soul to the devil." "But I," cried Hus, lifting up his eyes toward heaven, "do commit my spirit into thy hands, O Lord Jesus Christ."3

In the fifteenth and the sixteenth centuries many Reformation "protestants" were imprisoned or killed. Religious groups such as the Anabaptists, the Baptists, the Puritans, the Quakers, and others met persecution. Names like John Bunyan, Roger Williams, and Elijah Baker, from only a few centuries past, echo the Baptist struggle for religious liberty. Martyrdom is not an ancient matter either, however. Only a few years ago men like Dietrich Bonhoeffer, Bill Wallace, Martin Luther King, Jr., and others died for their beliefs. Many others were imprisoned in Nazi Germany, Communist China, or Russia. These joined the ranks of another company of sufferers—"for so persecuted they the prophets which went before you." The Bible bears witness to the persecution of Joseph, David, Elijah, Amos, Jeremiah, Stephen, Peter, Paul, and many others. Through it all they had become "more than conquerors through him who loved us" (Rom. 8:35-37).

Martin Niemoeller spent many months in the German concentration camps during World War II. When his minister father was asked about his reaction to this, he said; "Yes, it is a terrible thing to have a son in a concentration camp. . . . But there would be something more terrible for us: If God had needed a faithful martyr, and our Martin had been unwilling."[4] The loyal Christian does not seek trouble, nor desire injury, nor have a martyr complex, but stands ready to witness for the Lord no matter what the consequences may be.

Often people will say, "I can't talk about my faith; I'll just live it." Live it we must, of course, but we must also learn to talk about it and share our experience we have had in Christ with others. Keith Miller indicated how he came to realize that this notion that one could "live the faith and not talk about it" idea is totally "selfish." This way of thinking, Miller asserted, is like a man who has been ill with a dread disease and is now being secretly cured, who walks back into the disease ward from which he came and only seeks to make the other patients more comfortable rather than introducing them to the physician who can cure them.[5] Words, as well as actions, are essential to introduce someone to Christ.

Theodore P. Ferris told about a young Presbyterian minister who was pastor of a large church in one of our great industrial cities.[6] One of the most active and generous members of the church was a woman who was married to a prominent and wealthy man. The husband never came to church, or took any interest in it, or gave anything to it. Over the years the young minister became concerned about the wealthy man and decided he would make an appointment with him so they could talk about the matter. Later the young minister was admitted and sat across the desk from the older, austere man. In a very simple way he unfolded the Christian gospel and then said to the man: "I think you ought to do something about this one way or the other." When he finished, there was dead silence as the older man did not move or speak.

The young man proceeded to go over the gospel story again, emphasizing it a little more. Again he was met only by silence, and he began to wish he had never undertaken this particular mission. Nevertheless, he drew himself together and went through the story a third time. Again he was met only by absolute silence. He felt so uncomfortable that he longed for a way out of the room. Without speaking, the older man reached over and took a pad and wrote something on it and then passed it to him. The young minister read: "I am so deeply moved that I cannot speak." In all of his adult life, this was the first time anyone had ever presented him the Christian gospel in a frank, straightforward way. The man became a member of the church and an outstanding Christian leader in the city.

We can only wonder how many may never have committed their lives to Christ, primarily because no one has bothered to introduce them to the Christlike way. As someone has stated, "We must keep the faith, but not keep it to ourselves."

The Challenge to Be Different

Today it is difficult for us to realize how unpopular the gospel was to many in the first century. Paul noted the difficulty when he declared: "But we preach Christ crucified, unto the Jews a stumblingblock, and unto the Greeks foolishness" (1 Cor. 1:23). The Greek word translated *foolishness* might be better read with a stronger word, *obscenity.* Leslie Weatherhead describes a picture which was scribbled on a Roman wall in the early part of the first century. In this picture a man is depicted bowing down before a cross which has a figure hanging on it with the head of an ass. Underneath were written these words: "Alex, the Jew worships his God."[7] The early Christians were often met with ridicule, scorn, derision, and contempt. To be a Christian then was no easy matter. It required a loyal faith, deep love, great courage, strong convictions, and an inner assurance of life eternal. One had to be willing to be different.

The word *Christian* is found only three times in the New Testament, but in fifteen of the twenty-seven New Testament writings Christians are called *saints.* In writing to the Roman church, Paul declared: "To all that be in Rome, beloved of God, called to be saints" (Rom. 1:7, KJV). Paul's letters to the Corinthians, Colossians, Ephesians, and others are all directed to the saints in the churches. *Saint* was not a special term addressed to a unique group of pious individuals but was a word used to designate all Christians. A saint is not a perfect individual without sin but is one who is set apart and committed to the Christlike way. All Christians are saints because they are "in Christ," who is the "Holy One of God." The Christian is a saint, then, because he or she is committed to Christ and is called by Him to a life which is different because of His consecration.

To follow Jesus Christ has never been an easy task, and it is no different today. To stand up for the high ethical and moral principles which Christ wants us to follow may sometimes cause us problems or difficulties since the world around us is constantly trying to squeeze us into its mold. Although few of us may face death or violent persecution in following Christ today, we meet persecution of a more subtle kind, nevertheless. If we take our Christian faith seriously, we may be labeled a square, an oddball, a wet blanket, a spoilsport, a grind, or a prude. It is not easy to stay out of step with the crowd and be in step with Christ. Yet many Christians stand up for Christ daily.

I know one man who quit his job as manager of a restaurant rather than sell liquor. A young married woman spoke of changing jobs because her boss continued to make improper advances toward her. I know students who are willing to take a lower grade rather than cheat on a test. A young man told me that he dropped football when his coach continued to tell the boys that they had to play "dirty" in order to win. Young couples have changed apartments and acquired new friends rather than endanger their lives with neighbors who used drugs and sex for their "kicks."

The Christian, then, tries to keep in step with the drumbeat of Christ and does not allow the noise around him to pressure him into the path of conformity.

> I appeal to you therefore, brethren, by the mercies of God, to present your bodies as a living sacrifice, holy and acceptable to God, which is your spiritual worship. Do not be conformed to this world but be transformed by the renewal of your mind, that you may prove what is the will of God, what is good and acceptable and perfect (Rom. 12:1-2).

Myron Augsburger was asked one day if he had seen a painting which depicted the broad and the narrow ways of which Christ spoke. When he said yes, he was asked to describe it. He described a painting with the broad road leading downhill filled with people on it. The narrow road was over at the edge of the picture winding up a mountain to the golden city in the distance. "But that is wrong," his friend interrupted. "The narrow road is right in the middle of the broad road—just heading the other way."[8]

Augsburger had to agree. With their backs toward God, many travel the broad road away from God. Those seeking to follow God find that the narrow road often runs head-on into the stream of humanity going the wrong way.

To walk in His way is demanding, nevertheless the Christian takes the path of Christ unashamedly. We seek to "lay aside every weight, and sin which clings so closely," and run "with perseverance the race that is set before us, looking to Jesus the pioneer and perfecter of our faith, who for the joy that was set before him endured the cross, despising the shame, and is seated at the right hand of the throne of God" (Heb. 12:1-2). Jesus has vividly pictured the difficulty of following Him when He declared: "Enter by the narrow gate; for the gate is wide and the way is easy, that leads to destruction, and those who enter by it are many. For the gate is narrow and the way is hard, that leads to life, and those who find it are few" (Matt. 7:13-14).

Walking the narrow way is not only sometimes uncomfortable but often dangerous. Donald H. Tippett, a retired Methodist bishop, has one eye which is badly drooped. Ernest Campbell asked a friend on one occasion how Tippett received that kind of eye injury. The story and what follows are quite remarkable.[9] Years ago Tippett was a pastor in New York City. Two young men planned a robbery in upstate New York, and, in order to establish an alibi, they came by to visit the minister. While they were chatting with him, the pastor had to leave the room to take a telephone call in another room. The young men were fearful that he was suspicious of them, and they jumped him in his office and beat him so badly with brass knuckles that they mangled his left eye. Later when they were captured, he pleaded for the young men and got their sentences reduced. He visited them in prison and helped them plan their future. He helped support one of the young men through college and later through medical school. That young man is now an ophthalmologist. Although Tippett did not find the Christian way always easy or even safe, he has demonstrated through his life the power of Christian love along the narrow Way.

Take Up Your Cross

"If any man would come after me," Jesus said, "let him deny himself, and take up his cross and follow me" (Matt. 16:24). The cross has always been at the heart of the Christian faith. It stands for the worst humanity could do to God's great gift of Himself to us, and also represents, on the other hand, the highest revelation of the greatness of God's love. The German theologian Jürgen Moltmann, in his book *The Crucified God,* noted that the crucified Christ in His own time was regarded as a scandal and as foolishness and that in our time to put the cross in the center of our faith is considered old-fashioned. But he boldly asserted that if the church of Christ and our theology about him are to be biblical and genuine, then the crucified Christ must be the essential emphasis of our faith. "In Christianity," he insisted "the cross is the test of everything which deserves to be called Christian."[10]

The cross is not something that many of us want as a part of our life-style. We had rather sing about the "old rugged cross on a hill far away." We like the cross at a distance. When it gets too close to us, we begin to shuffle uncomfortably. In a time which has been characterized as the "age of the shrug," it is difficult to get many to shoulder a cross and move into the marketplace of life with it. Every follower of Christ is called to crucify selfishness and follow a higher calling—the way of Christ. Is this not what Dietrich Bonhoeffer meant in his famous statement? "When Christ calls a man, He bids him come and die."[11] Paul expressed it this way: "I have been crucified with

Christ; it is no longer I who live, but Christ who lives in me; and the life I now live in the flesh I live by faith in the Son of God, who loved me and gave himself for me" (Gal. 2:20).

No matter what else we might say about what constitutes being a Christian, the essential fact is that he or she is one who has come to Christ. It takes an effort of my own will, a personal commitment of my life to Him. I commit my life to Christ and say that I am going to walk His way and live for Him. No one says it will be easy, especially Christ. When we have committed our life to Christ, then it is not for sale to the cheaper offers which attract us. We have been bought with a price, and we are aware that the deepest insights into our own hearts come from what we are willing to make sacrifices for.

No Christian life, nor church, is true to the teaching of its Lord if it lives only for itself. We have been called to be used, to minister, to spend ourselves in service for the Christ. In the upper room Jesus took a towel and basin and washed the feet of each disciple when each of them felt the task beneath him. By the power of this example, Jesus indicated the nature of Christian discipleship—humble, selfless service. Jesus by His life, teachings, and death embodied the principle of sacrificial love. Christ has called us to imitate Him in our thoughts and actions. "For I have given you an example, that ye should do as I have done to you" (John 13:15, KJV). Taking up our cross involves the willingness to follow His example of costly love. A few, like Paul, Francis of Assisi, David Livingstone, Albert Schweitzer, Tom Dooley, and others have reflected on a worldwide scale this kind of dedication. Christians can strive to reflect this same kind of commitment where we live, work, play, and worship.

"I saw that the Church cannot be the Church," Keith Miller noted, "without a company of men and women with drastically changed purposes and directions, deeply motivated to be a servant people devoted to the Lord. I also saw that the evangelical awakening cannot become a mature reformation until it leads people into the brokenness and alienation of the secular world."[12]

In Alan Paton's novel, *Cry, the Beloved Country,* a native who was among the persecuted people of South Africa, declared: "I have never thought that a Christian would be free of suffering. . . . For our Lord suffered. And I came to believe that he suffered, not to save us from suffering, but to teach us how to bear suffering. For he knew there is no life without suffering."[13] The Christian, then, follows his Lord aware that to do so may sometimes cause misunderstanding, ridicule, or hostility. Our persecution may not be so severe as some in the past. For us it may take the form of being passed over for a promotion, not receiving an invitation to certain parties or functions, losing an election, being snubbed at the office or school, or simply by being treated with a distant coolness. Some today, nevertheless, do suffer real persecution even if it is not physical. Many who take stands for unpopular causes often have to pay for it dearly.

Elton Trueblood has reminded us that many of the figures which Jesus used like salt, light, keys, leaven, fire, bread, and water represent some kind of penetration. Salt penetrates meat to preserve it; light penetrates darkness; bread penetrates the body to nourish it, and so forth. The basic purpose of the Christian, then is to penetrate the world with the power of his sacrificial witness. Jesus sends us out into the world as His disciples to be the transforming force in society. Our worship must not remain within the walls of a church building but most touch all of our life. "If the witness is to penetrate, as our culture requires, the major witness must be made not in the church but in the world."[14]

In the novel, *The Trampled Cross*, by Joseph Hocking, a British soldier fell into the hands of the Arabs during a time of desert fighting. The Arabian chieftain placed two sticks in the form of a cross and says to the officer: "There is the symbol of your Faith. Trample on it, and we shall let you go free."[15] Will we as Christians trample upon the cross by the way we live or will we instead take up our cross and follow Christ?

The promised benediction for the persecuted is "For great is your reward in heaven" (Matt. 5:12, KJV). To serve Christ with a motive for reward is an unworthy, selfish desire and does not entail an understanding of the nature of any of the Beatitudes (1 Cor. 13:3). The word *result* rather than *reward* might depict more clearly the meaning of this promise. The result of taking up one's cross and following Christ enables one to share in the great company of dedicated witnesses and martyrs who live on, not only in our memory, but eternally in the presence and glory of God (Rom. 8:38-39).

I recently heard a man state that "All dedication stems from selfishness. A person does something for another just because it makes him feel good." I think that is hardly ever true and cannot begin to account for the sacrifices which many make in the name of Christ. Out of the trauma of the Second World War came a volume entitled *Burma Diary*. Written in 1942, this book described the flight of civilians and soldiers from Burma to avoid the advancing Japanese army. Paul Geren, a refugee professor from the University of Rangoon, wrote in his diary about the filthy job facing them in attempting to move the patients, many of whom were suffering from dysentery, out of one hospital into another one. The endless rains and the inability to get clothing and bed linens dry made the assignments even more difficult. "A reeking stench like a burnt offering to some perverse deity," the author observed, "rose from the patients, the soiled bedding, and soiled clothing."

He, along with an American who had joined the British army before the United States got into the war, and a British soldier, stood looking at the ordeal which awaited them. "I am very glad at this moment," the American said to the British soldier, "that I am an agnostic."

"Since he did not believe in the love of Christ, he could leave the handling of these dysentery victims to the sweepers," Professor Geren observed. "Since his friend did believe in it, he was not free to stand by and watch. Nor was I," he affirmed. "Get down in it! Pick the patients up! . . . There is no need to call this filthiness sweet, or to start enjoying it through a strange inversion. Only one thing is necessary: for love's sake it must be done."[16]

That's the Christlike spirit—"to march into hell for a heavenly cause." Sometimes the Christian's work may be dirty, nasty, difficult, or repulsive, but he or she does not turn from it simply because it is not easy or sweet. Why? "The love of Christ constrains us." As Paul has written, "For it has been granted to you that for the sake of Christ you should not only believe in him but also suffer for his sake" (Phil. 1:29).

Are the Beatitudes an impossible goal or unrealistic ideal? Dietrich Bonhoeffer struggled with the same dilemma and concluded:

> Having reached the end of the beatitudes, we naturally ask if there is any place on this earth for the community which they describe. Clearly, there is one place, and only one, and that is where the poorest, meekest, and most sorely tried of all men is to be found—on the cross at Golgotha. The fellowship of the beatitudes is the fellowship of the Crucified. With him it has lost all, and with him it has found all. From the cross there comes the call

"blessed, blessed." The last beatitude is addressed directly to the disciples, for only they can understand it. . . .[17]

Notes

1. Harry Emerson Fosdick, *Successful Christian Living* (New York: Harper & Brothers, 1937), p. 81.

2. M. Gabriel Marcel, *The Mystery of Being* (London: Harvill Press, 1950), Vol. II, pp. 125-145.

3. Matthew Spinka, *John Hus: A Biography* (Princeton N.J.: Princeton University Press, 1968), p. 288.

4. Ernest Trice Thompson, *The Sermon on the Mount and Its Meaning for Today* (Richmond, Va.: John Knox Press, 1961), p. 37.

5. Keith Miller, *The Taste of New Wine* (Waco, Tex.: Word Books, 1965), p. 89.

6. Theodore P. Ferris, *The Interpreter's Bible,* edited by George Buttrick (New York: Abingdon-Cokesbury Press, 1954), Vol. IX, p. 117.

7. Leslie Weatherhead, *That Immortal Sea* (New York: Abingdon Press, 1953), p. 180.

8. Myron Augsburger, *The Expanded Life* (Nashville: Abingdon Press, 1972), p. 103.

9. Ernest T. Campbell, "The Church and the Common Good," (An unpublished sermon delivered in the Riverside Church, New York City, New York, October 12, 1975), p. 7.

10. Jürgen Moltmann, *The Crucified God* (New York: Harper & Row, 1974), p. 7.

11. Dietrich Bonhoeffer, *The Cost of Discipleship* (London: SCM Press, Ltd, 1959), p. 79.

12. Keith Miller, *A Second Touch* (Waco, Tex.: Word Books, 1967), pp. 115-116.

13. Alan Paton, *Cry, the Beloved Country* (New York: Charles Scribner's Sons, 1948), p. 227.

14. Elton Trueblood, *The Company of the Committed* (New York: Harper & Row, 1961), p. 90.

15. Cited in A. Leonard Griffith, *Beneath the Cross of Jesus* (Nashville: Abingdon Press, 1961), pp. 67-68.

16. Paul Geren, *Burma Diary* (New York: Harper & Brothers, 1943), pp. 51-52.

17. Bonhoeffer, p. 103.

We must remember that the symbol of the church is not the life-extending apparatus of the geriatric ward, but the cross. And the goal of the church is not self-preservation, but self-giving."

—James W. Cox *Surprised by God.*

9

The Forgotten Beatitude

It is more blessed to give than to receive (Acts 20:35).

In his departing words to the Ephesian Christian leaders at the port of Miletus, the apostle Paul cited one of the sayings of Jesus which has not been preserved in the Gospels. The only other place Paul quoted Jesus directly is found in 1 Corinthians 11:24-25 where he is describing the Lord's Supper. There are a number of places in his Epistles where he alluded to sayings of Jesus, but he did not quote them directly.[1] When Paul delivered his speech, the Gospels had not yet been written, but he was familiar with the sayings and teachings of Jesus which were passed on from one Christian group to another by word of mouth. Later, after writing his Gospel, John observed that there were so many other things which Jesus said and did, that if they were written down, the world could not contain all the books which would be written (John 21:25). The Gospels could not possibly include every word and deed of Jesus.

Paul's hearers were obviously familiar with this saying for he admonished them with the word *remember*. For them it was not an unknown Beatitude. He simply reminded them to fall back upon one of the sayings of Jesus which had been treasured up in the memory of the early disciples. Paul recounted this Beatitude with the assurance that it was known to the Christian community gath-

183

ered before him. He entreated them to remember it on this occasion.

Paul's farewell speech poured forth like that of a pastor whose heart was filled with love and devotion for his people. He reminded them of his public ministry of teaching and his personal house-to-house visitation. His ministry had not been easy but was filled with trials and tears. Nevertheless, he had spoken fearlessly. He had supported himself by his own hands so he would not be dependent upon others and could give generously to them. He had exemplified by his life what he had taught. He told them that he would probably not see them again, but he felt compelled to go to Jerusalem to fulfill what he sensed the purpose of God was for him. He then charged them to be aware of the dangers within and without the church from those who wanted to destroy it. He warned them to preserve their own spiritual life and to nourish the people they were responsible for guiding.

Later Ephesus and other churches in Asia Minor would experience the bloody persecution of Domitian and struggle with the heresies of the Nicolaitans and gnosticism. When Paul finished speaking, he prayed for them and they embraced him and wept. Paul had labored longer in Ephesus than any other place, and he had grown to love these friends. In this brief passage we see Paul not as a great theologian, or a great preacher, but simply as a loving pastor.

In this tender moment Paul reached back in his memory of the teachings of Jesus to leave with them some saying that would guide them. They had no New Testament. The Gospels had not been written. Most of them probably could not read anyway. Suddenly Paul recalled the words. The use of double emphatic personal pronouns in the Greek text emphasized that Paul affirmed that these words were from Jesus. "Remember how *he himself* said

. . . (author's words & italics)." In this unforgettable sentence of Jesus, "It is more blessed to give than to receive," Paul presented a summary of the Lord's teachings. This golden saying casts its light upon the pathway for those who would follow Jesus, and it offers light and guidance for those who would travel in that direction.

It would be interesting to know the occasion of this Beatitude. Did Jesus utter it after the poor widow dropped in her mite at the Temple? Did He express it after the meal in the house of Zacchaeus when Zacchaeus stated that half of his goods he would give to the poor, and if he had defrauded anyone, he would restore fourfold? Did Jesus relay these words softly to His disciples as the rich young ruler walked away sorrowfully? Were they said with flashing eyes after the mother of James and John had tried to secure a special place in Christ's kingdom? Were they spoken tenderly after Jesus Himself had washed the disciples' feet? Were they voiced in anger to Simon after he had refused to wash the dust from Jesus' feet, and a woman had anointed them with ointment from an alabaster flask and then wiped them with her hair?

We do not know the setting. They may have been words said privately to His disciples or in a public sermon. Although we do not know the occasion, the sentence, "It is more blessed to give than to receive" still calls us back to the heart of the Christian faith. Unfortunately, we have reduced and hidden them only to be spoken before or after the offering in our worship services. But if we link these words only to our money, we may have missed the original thrust. This Beatitude summarizes Christian living, not just financial giving. It focuses on attitude, a way of life, a philosophy of living. *The New English Bible* translates the verse this way: "Happiness lies more in the giving than in receiving." This Beatitude points us toward the path that leads to real happiness.

The Blessing of Receiving

"It is more blessed to give than to receive." The use of the phrase *more blessed* implies that there is a blessing in receiving. Our capacity to receive in a real sense determines our ability to give. If we do not understand the blessing of receiving, the higher blessing of giving will also elude us. Giving and receiving are not depicted as merely opposite sides of a coin. The comparison seems to suggest a difference between a higher and lower form of blessing. One is obviously greater and more important, but that does not indicate that the lesser has no value or significance. There is more blessedness in giving, but receiving carries with it a dimension of blessedness also. "Freely ye have received, freely give" (Matt. 10:8, KJV).

While I was in college and seminary, I had the privilege of serving as pastor of Good Hope Baptist Church, a rural church in northern Virginia. Although many years have passed since that time, I retain many delightful memories from my ministry there and have continued to stay in touch with that fine Christian community. One summer when we were having our annual church revival, the guest minister and I were visiting various members in the community. We had completed a nice visit with one of the poorer families in the community and walked to the front porch to leave. The lady of the house turned to me and said, "I have a bag of apples I would like to give you, Pastor."

I very graciously said, "Thanks. I appreciate that but I don't know how we could keep them right now."

As we got into the car to drive away, my friend Al said to me: "Bill, that was a mistake."

"What was?" I asked.

"When that lady offered you the apples," Al said, "you should have taken them. Although she was poor, she was still trying to share something with you out of her generous spirit and to show you some small appreciation for your ministry here."

He was right. In my youthful response I may have made the giver feel that her small gift was not worthy. Of course, I had not intended that. I was more concerned with where I could keep the apples later so they would not spoil. But I had missed the main point. Well, I have never forgotten that lesson and have tried to learn how to be a more gracious receiver through the years.

Most of us will have to admit, if we are really being honest, that we have difficulty in receiving. I always shuffle my feet and get tongue-tied if someone extends a compliment to me. Congratulations often leave me open-mouthed and feeling awkward. Upon receiving a gift, I often struggle with words which seem to communicate in only a clumsy way my real feelings of appreciation. Many of us receive with the lumbering grace of a hippopotamus. Our inability to accept praise often offends or rejects the person who is seeking to be gracious to us. This might really reflect more about our own insecurity and fears than we would like to admit even to ourselves.

Keith Miller related an experience which he had right after he had just given a talk in his church. A man whom he respected very much affirmed him enthusiastically with the compliment, "That was a great job, Keith!"

"Thanks, but I'm afraid I was too direct!" Miller replied. "I was tired and felt a little hostile." His friend looked at him strangely and then walked away into the educational wing of the church.

In an instant, Miller knew what he had done. His friend had sincerely tried to express his appreciation. But instead of accepting his affirmation, Miller's actions told him that he was not really very smart because Miller picked up some negative things about the talk which his friend didn't hear. He realized that his negative response had in fact rejected his friend and the kindness which he had expressed through his praise. Miller, of course, had not meant to do that. "Never before had I realized fully the negative, squelching effect of refusing to accept another's kind words."[2]

A gift is indeed enriched or degraded by its reception. Anne Morrow Lindbergh wrote several years ago about an unforgettable character she knew named Edward Sheldon. "He knew how to receive so graciously," she said, "that the gift was enhanced by its reception. It was the rarest pleasure to bring things to him . . . warmed by his welcome, how beautiful became the things one brought to him."[3] Unfortunately, not many of us are like that. To receive graciously from someone who gives to us is, in reality, sharing a gift of ourself with them. It is wrong merely to assume that the giver will know we are appreciative of the gift. We all know what a warm embrace, a sincere handshake, a thank-you note, or a phone call means to us when we have been the one who gave.

David Dunn was correct. There really is "a gracious art of receiving." He spoke about a niece of his that he felt had completely mastered the art of receiving compliments. "Giving her a compliment," he said, "is always an enjoyable experience." First, she gives a quick smile of appreciation, along with a equally quick "Thank-you." This is then followed by a comment that takes the focus off herself. She might reply, for example by saying: "Yes, isn't it a pretty dress? Mother sent it to me." On another occasion she replied: "I got the idea for rearranging the room from so-and-so's new book on interior decorating." Her secret is clear. She has learned to accept the compliments only for a fleeting second and then passes them on to others.[4]

Many things are missed in life because we have not

learned how to receive them. I might fill my house with books, but unless they are read they are not really received. I might walk through an art gallery filled with famous paintings, but without some sense of art appreciation I cannot receive what they offer. I may have hundreds of cassette tapes of classical music, but without some capacity to appreciate their quality I cannot receive them. I might enroll in a university and attend classes, but unless I am willing to receive knowledge which my teachers will impart I cannot learn. Receiving is not easy. The best things are not acquired quickly or effortlessly. Before something is received into my life, I must have the capacity to welcome and admit its presence.

This means that I cannot remain neutral. Receiving is an act which requires response on my part. I do not really receive something if I am unwilling to accept it. Several years ago when I was traveling through the Bavarian mountains, I noticed that outside many of the houses the owners had placed large barrels to collect rainwater. The containers received the water so it might be used later. In a sense every life needs to be a container to receive. Without the act of reception, the gifts which are offered to me cannot be mine. Before the prodigal son could begin to receive, he had to return home. If he had remained in the far country, he would not have experienced his father's forgiveness.

One of the characters of the New Testament who struggled with his inability to receive was the rich young ruler. "Good Teacher, what must I do to inherit eternal life?" (Mark 10:17). Here within this young man were two forces at war. On the one hand, he thought he had to earn his eternal life. And on the other hand, he spoke of it as though it were a gift—an inheritance. Like too many today, the rich young ruler thought he had to earn or achieve his salvation. He had to give away something, not achieve something, and enter a life of service by following Him.

Salvation is a gift. At the very heart of the Christian faith is receiving. The gift of God is eternal life. It is a gift. The first Bible verse which most of us learn states, "For God so loved the world that he gave his only Son, that whoever believes in him should not perish but have eternal life" (John 3:16). Salvation is a gift. It is given by God. The root of most of the church's heresies has been the effort of men and women to earn their salvation rather than to receive it as God's loving gift. Remember the apostle Paul's ringing affirmation: "For by grace you have been saved through faith; and this is not your own doing, it is the gift of God—not because of works, lest any man should boast" (Eph. 2:8-9).

So much of what we have in life comes to us as a gift. The world with its sunshine and rain, night and day, summer and winter, springtime and harvest, comes to us as a gift from the Creator. Our very life came to us as a gift from our parents. We had no design in it. The wealth under our feet in the earth's crust and the riches buried beneath the depths are gifts from the boundless provisions of nature. We are stewards of the earth, not its masters. We can appreciate the earth's bounty, discover it, utilize it, consume it, but first we must receive it.

In our churches, many of us are debtors to the people who generations before us gave sacrificially so we might worship in comfort today. We enjoy the benefits paid for by their foresight and willingness to give. When you sit in a church building which is over fifty years old, remember you are a receiver. You are a receiver of the thoughts, plans, efforts, and gifts of those who were here before you. None of us is independent. We are receivers all. We are receivers of electricity and telephones, heat and air-conditioning, automobiles and airplanes, radio and television, papers and books, houses and farms. We are the recipients of experiments, inventions, discoveries, explorations, and sacrifices of countless thousands through the course of history. We are debtors to them for their innumerable gifts, too countless to name. We stand on their shoulders of accomplishment and have received more than we ever could repay.

Years ago a wealthy student who was attending Williams College was accused of defacing some of the college property. When he came in to see the college president, Mark Hopkins, he arrogantly whipped out his checkbook and asked how much was it going to cost him to pay for the damages. President Hopkins ordered the young man to sit down and exclaimed: "No man can pay for what he receives here. Can you pay for the sacrifice of Colonel Williams who founded the college? Can you pay for the half-paid professors who have remained here to teach when they could have gone elsewhere? Every student here is a charity case!" How often all of us forget that.

My debt is so great because I have received from so many. So have we all. I am indebted to my parents for things which they did for me that I can still remember and for many more that I can no longer recall. But I am indebted to countless teachers, friends, neighbors, farmers, butchers, bakers, ministers, builders, electricians, plumbers, politicians, and endless others. We all receive so much from so many different hands. I cannot possibly receive all these benefits and sacrifices without a sense of indebtedness and gratitude. Like Paul I must declare: "I am under obligation both to Greeks and to barbarians, both to the wise and to the foolish" (Rom. 1:14).

Love involves the gift of receiving. Love is not something that can be demanded, forced, or bribed. I cannot demand that my wife love me. Nor can I make my children love me. I first give love to them, and they receive it from me, and in return they express love to me. Love is a gift. It is a gift given in relationships which cannot be bought or earned.

It is a blessing indeed to receive the grace of God. God's salvation comes as a gift. We cannot earn it nor do we merit it. We receive it as gift. Only those who have experienced the forgiveness of sins can really understand the significance of receiving. To receive the grace of God is to know the great joy of being accepted by God. Those who have passed through a spiritual experience in which they have moved from darkness to light, from bondage to freedom, from the depths of poverty to the "unsearchable riches in Christ" can know how to give graciously. "Thanks be to God for his inexpressible gift!" (2 Cor. 9:15). These are the words of Paul who had known great forgiveness. Paul became a great giver because he had received so much. Paul gave thanks to God "without ceasing" and his actions kept peace with his words.

We Christians give of ourselves because we have received so much from God. The extent of God's giving reached to Calvary. Drawn to the love of the Christ who gave His life for us, we seek to follow His lead in sacrificial giving. Our lives have been changed. They have been changed by the very acceptance (receiving) of forgiveness itself, and we are radically different within because of God's loving grace. We give not because we must, but because we want to express our joy at receiving so great a love. We cannot receive God's great gift and keep it to ourselves. We are compelled to share it. As we have received, so we give and share with others. And the paradox is that as we give, we also enable ourselves to receive. "Every one to whom much is given," Jesus said, "of him will much be required" (Luke 12:48).

The Greater Blessing of Giving

"It is more blessed to give than to receive." These words from Jesus are at the very heart of His teachings. They are a great living principle which directs His followers to a higher way of life. Even after two thousand years, however, these words still seem to cut against the grain. They sound nice when the minister uses them when the offering is collected for the worship hour, but as a principle for daily living, someone may remark quickly, they seem hopelessly idealistic. It is a hard saying. These words move against the current stream in modern society. Voices by the hundreds or thousands counsel us to get, earn, win, procure, save, and secure. The prudent, thrifty, and industrious individuals are lifted up as models. This sentence sounds unnatural. Why, it strikes at the basic instinct for self-preservation!

Jesus knew that. Like so many of His teachings, this one called His followers to a higher standard than self-centeredness and self-preservation. This sentence is lifted up like a blazing torch in a dark world to shed light on a path that leads away from the crowded streets to a level of walking on a higher road. Jesus knew that this attitude toward life could not be for those who wanted the easy way. He called His disciples to walk in the narrow way which leads to abundant life.

Generosity finds its source in the Christian not in natural instincts but arises from within persons who have been redeemed and inspired by God's marvelous grace. The self-giving spirit cannot be lifted out of its environment and be expected to live. It arises out of a life rooted and grounded in the rich soil of forgiveness, thanksgiving, joy, gratitude, and commitment. The fine, delicate virtue of self-giving love cannot be grown in lean soil. Rich soil is essential for its survival and growth. Paul's prayer for the early Christians reflected this view.

> And that Christ may dwell in your hearts through faith; that you, being rooted and grounded in love, may have power to comprehend with all the saints what is the breadth and length and height and depth, and to know the love of Christ which surpasses knowledge, that you may be filled with all the fulness of God (Eph. 3:17-19).

And again he noted: "As therefore you received Christ Jesus the Lord, so live in him, rooted and built up in him and established in the faith, just as you were taught, abounding in thanksgiving" (Col. 2::6-7).

Many seek to harvest generosity out of meager spiritual soil and they produce a thin level of giving which is done reluctantly and grudgingly. Many of these people give only from a sense of social compulsion. "Others are doing it, and I will be ostracized by my friends and neighbors if I do not." These persons often weigh the possible responses and calculate the reactions of others before they give. There are some whose selfishness has pushed them into being stingy and close-fisted.

Raymond Balcomb wrote about a wealthy man who had never been very generous in his giving. His church was having a building program and the financial compaign committee appointed a special committee to study his case and determine the best way to approach him. When the committee finally visited him, they stated that in light of his resources they were sure he would want to make a substantial contribution to his church.

"I see that you have considered it all quite carefully," he said. "In the course of your investigation did you discover that I have an aged, widowed mother who has no other means of support?" No, they were not aware of that. "Did you know that I have a sister who was left by a drunken husband with five small children and no means of providing for them?" No, they did not know that. "Did you know that I have a brother who was crippled in an accident and will never be able to do another day's work in his life to support himself and his family?" The committee, obviously feeling miserable by now, had to state that they were also unaware of this. "Well," he exclaimed triumphantly, "I've never done anything for them, so why should I do anything for you?"[5]

Why should he? Why should he learn to give? He needs to get outside his selfishness and discover the joy and blessing of helping others in need. He needs to discover the inner peace and sense of genuine accomplishment which comes in giving. Why should he give? He gives so he might experience the rejoinder which is set loose by unselfish acts. He gives to unlock the door of hoarding and keeping to let in the spirit of compassion, love, tenderness, benevolence, and unselfishness. He gives to enlarge his life, to redefine his attitude toward others and himself, to embrace a nobler way of behavior, to multiply the work of his own hands. To give is to experience the higher way of loving. Why should he give? He gives in response to the cries of pain, disease, grief, loneliness, and alienation which have reached his ears. He gives because he has seen the effects of war, hatred, prejudice, injustice, and oppression, and he wants to make a better world. He gives in response to a vision of a different kind of world when sacrificial love is its foundation. He gives because he has learned a more blessed way.

Unfortunately everyone does not give for noble reasons. Some give out of fear of reprehension, censure, rebuke, embarrassment, or reluctantly. One such man wrote the Internal Revenue Department and explained: "Dear Sir: Five years ago I cheated on my income tax, and I am enclosing twenty-five dollars in cash because I cannot sleep well at nights. If I still can't sleep well at nights, I will send the remainder." It was unsigned, of course. I wonder how many people spend sleepless nights because of money. Many toss and turn sleeplessly because of the way they earn it, spend it, count it, bank it, bet it, invest it, and borrow it. I wonder how many are sleepless because of the way they give it? "Money as a master is man's worst master," observed George W. Truett. "Money as a servant is one of man's most valuable servants."[6]

At the heart of our problem with giving, and this includes our attitude toward money but much more, is our basic sin of selfishness. Life is looked at too much through the glasses marked *me, mine, my,* and *I.* Giving will always be done reluctantly and grudgingly when it is seen as a threat to what one must give up of his or her own desires.

In the parable of the rich man who wanted to build bigger and better barns (Luke 12:16-21), he is not condemned by Jesus because he was dishonest or heartless. He is called a fool because he wanted to use what he had in a foolish way. He planned to eat, drink, and be merry. In this brief story a dozen of the words show that the focus of the man was upon himself. "*I* will do this," "*I* will store," "*I* will say," "*my* crops," "*my* barns," "*my* grain," "*my* goods," "*my* soul." He only thought about *his* rights, needs, and desires. He was concerned only about himself. The final test for him was not the size of his barns but the quality of his inner life.

But that man has a twin brother and sister on nearly every block, doesn't he? He/she is in our homes, churches, schools, offices, factories, banks, stores, and government. He/she is the officer of our club, the head of the board, chairman of our committees, director of our finances, and in every place you look. He/she is everywhere. He/she is in each of us.

Self-centeredness eats away at one's personhood, destroying its potential for becoming its real self. The Dead Sea is dead because it has no outlet. Water flows in but cannot flow out. Therefore, it is lifeless. Our lives are like the Dead Sea when we are only on the receiving end and are unwilling to share. We are spiritually dead. A clenched fist never receives; only as a hand opens and gives can it in turn receive. This Beatitude challenges the Christian to direct one's life outward and not inward. An old epitaph affirms this truth. "What I kept I lost. What I gave I kept!"

A person has reached a level of real maturity when he or she accepts some responsibility for others in society. No one lives as an island apart from the rest of mankind. In 1935 the Mayo brothers gave a generous gift to the University of Minnesota for a graduate medical facility. Dr. William J. Mayo wrote a letter that was sent with the gift. Here is a brief excerpt from the letter: "Our father recognized certain definite social obligations. He believed that any man who had better opportunity than others—greater strength of mind, body, or character, owed something to those who had not been so provided; that is that the important thing in life is not to accomplish for oneself alone, but for each to carry his share of collective responsibility."[7] As Jesus said, "Every one to whom much is given, of him will much be required" (Luke 12:48).

"Humanity always crowds the audience-room when God holds court," Walter Rauschenbusch once wrote.[8] The Christian cannot escape responsibility for reaching out to others. Jesus took the two great Commandments (Lev. 19:18; Deut. 6:5) and put them together and made them one. "You shall love the Lord your God with all your heart, and with all your soul, and with all your mind. This is the great and first commandment. And a second is like it, You shall love your neighbor as yourself" (Matt. 22:37-

39). Love toward God and other persons are bound together. The love that we experience in God's grace is indeed an intensely personal matter, but it can never be only a private matter. I am not an isolated ego. Love for God must always issue outward in love toward others. To say "I couldn't care less" about other people and their needs is to walk out of step with Jesus. Our life reflects love toward God by extending love unselfishly toward others. Our religion and morality cannot be separated.

It is impossible to love God in an abstract way. We show our love toward Him in and through the way we relate to other persons. The Epistle First John gives a description of our love toward God. "If any one says, 'I love God,' and hates his brother, he is a liar; for he who does not love his brother whom he has seen, cannot love God whom he has not seen. And this commandment we have from him, that he who loves God should love his brother also" (1 John 4:20-21). To say that I love God means little, if I am unwilling to show this love in my attitude and dealing with others.

Our love of God takes shape as we love others in particular places and at specific times. As we give ourselves to others, we give to God. It is more blessed to give because it moves us out of our self-centeredness into the needs of others. In His description of the last judgment, Jesus indicated vividly that the Godlike persons will be those who have demonstrated their love for God by ministering to the hungry, the strangers, the sick, the poor, and others in need (Matt. 25:31-46). "Truly, I say to you, as you did it to one of the least of these my brethren, you did it to me" (v. 40).

Because we Christians have known such magnanimous love, we, too, must love. It will not be easy. To give is costly. Giving costs time, thought, money, commitment, living, and sometimes dying. The sacrifices may be large or small. The Christian has learned to love and give even when the recipient cannot reciprocate. Christian giving goes out of its way to help others as God's grace does for us. Jesus called His followers to love those who have not earned or deserved love. This self-giving love challenges us to reach out to the difficult, hostile, unloving, or even our enemies (Luke 6:32-36). This kind of love does not give because it is attracted to these persons. It does not give expecting something in response but gives in order to help the other person. Self-giving love reaches out because there is a need and an opportunity to minister. It does not seek recognition or reward.

A number of years ago, in a church where I was serving as pastor, one of the members took the responsibility of caring for an elderly woman in the congregation who had no family to assist her. This woman was very gracious with both her time and attention. Each week she would buy groceries for her, baked cakes or pies, and would stop by often to talk with her and see if she needed anything. The elderly lady, unfortunately, was a very grouchy and disagreeable person that no one could satisfy very easily. One day, after the generous woman had had a difficult time with the elderly lady, her husband asked her: "Why in the world do you fool with Mrs. Blank? She doesn't appreciate anything you do for her."

"No, she doesn't," the Christian woman responded. "But I don't do it to be appreciated." That is the spirit of this Beatitude. She assisted because she saw a need, and she did not expect a reward. To serve in the Master's name is compensation enough. It is the greater blessing of giving. To give is to receive.

Love cannot exist in a vacuum. If it is real, it will manifest itself in thought and action, reflection and flesh, word and deed. Real love is self-giving, not self-constraining. Real love reaches out; it does not ask to be coddled. Love gives itself. Love merges its being with its action. Love forgets self and extends itself into the needs of others. Love is self-expressing, not self-seeking. The Christian gives not because he or she has to but because they want to. This Christlike love is not merely a sentiment, but extended hands into the hurt of society. "It is more blessed to give than to receive." This is not just an abstract idea but a concrete principle for living. Is this not Paul's powerful theme in 1 Corinthians 13? Love is at the center of all the Christian's thinking, living, and ministering.

"It is more blessed to give than to receive" because it is more Christlike than anything we can do. In describing His ministry Jesus declared: "For the Son of man also came not to be served but to serve, and to give his life as a ransom for many" (Mark 10:45). The foundation for this Beatitude grew out of the example of Jesus who gave. God gave in His act of creation. He gave in His incarnation. He gave in love and self-sacrifice. The self-giving principles by which Jesus lived inevitably led to His death. But His death revealed and climaxed the very principles which He had taught. From Bethlehem to Calvary, from His birth to His death, the life of Jesus exemplified the Beatitude, "It is more blessed to give than to receive." Paul expressed it this way, "Though he was rich, yet for your sake he became poor, so that by his poverty you might become rich" (2 Cor. 8:9). In another place he wrote: "Though he was in the form of God, did not count equality with God a thing to be grasped, but emptied himself, taking the form of a servant, . . . and being found in human form he humbled himself and became obedient unto death, even death on a cross" (Phil. 2:6-8).

One of the most distinctive emphases in the Gospels is the concern and compassion which Jesus showed for the poor, the disadvantaged, and the sinful. Again and again, by word and deed, Jesus crossed the barriers separating sinners from the religious establishment and offered them forgiveness of sin and acceptance with God. He declared that his ministry was "to preach good news to the poor. . . . To proclaim release to the captives and, . . . to set at liberty those who are oppressed" (Luke 4:18). Jesus moved in and challenged customs and traditions which were put before people. Whenever customs or traditions demeaned or damaged a person, Jesus criticized them. His first priority was persons, not systems. He reached out to the blind, deaf, crippled, sick, and hurting. He touched the leper, the dead, the unclean, the demon possessed, and self-confessed sinners. Jesus touched the untouchable! But He had come to minister—"to give his life a ransom for many." Jesus did not just talk about giving. He lived it. The cross of Christ was the climax of a life which had been giving to others. His death was the logical outcome of the way he had lived—self-giving. "Greater love has no man than this, that a man lay down his life for his friends" (John 15:13). God so loved—what a Giver!

Christians have experienced His forgiveness, known His grace, received His mercy, and welcomed His compassion. For God so loved is a supreme blessing for which the Christian can only say: "Thanks be to God for his inexpressible gift!" (2 Cor. 9:15). But the Christian is obligated to do more than receive God's love. He or she is challenged to love even as he or she has been loved. "This is my commandment," Jesus said, "that you love one another as I have loved you" (John 15:12).

Jesus has called His followers to a higher law than the maxim: "Self-preservation is the first law of nature." Selfishness is self-love misdirected. To love oneself in the biblical sense is to fulfill the potential for which God has created us. Proper self-love demands a healthy respect for one's own personhood. Self-respect arises out of the awareness that we have been created in the "image of

God." In the Christian, self-love constantly denies itself so the higher self, which God has called us to be, might grow and advance. "For whoever would save his life," Jesus declared in a paradoxical statement, "will lose it; and whoever loses his life for my sake, he will save it" (Luke 9:24). The emphasis is not on how much a person can *get* out of life but on how much one can *give*. Life is not to be hoarded for self but is to be spent in service for Christ. "The self-sacrifice of the Redeemer was to be the living principle and law of the self-devotion of His people."[9] "It is more blessed to give than to receive." I like even better the translation of this verse by W. O. Carver. "It is blessed rather to be a giver than to be a getter."[10]

When Ernest Hemingway was given the medal for his Nobel prize for literature, he gave it to a church in Santiago. "You really do not feel you own something," he said, "until you can give it away." Do we really possess anything until we have the courage to give it away? Christ has taught us how to share as we have received the love he lived and died to give us. His call may lead us down familiar streets or along unknown paths. He may challenge us to greet strangers or friends. His way may sometimes be joyful, and at other times difficult. The response may sometimes be rewarded, and on other occasions discouraging. But He has promised to be with us (Matt. 28:-20).

Jesse Lyons once told about the discussions which they used to have in Richard Niebuhr's ethics class at Yale Seminary about what a person should do on the ocean if there were only provisions for four people and six people were in a lifeboat. They argued about who should die: the sick, the old, the well, the young? Clark Poling was a student in the class, and he debated heatedly the question with the rest. At the sound of the bell, Dr. Niebuhr would say, "We will continue this next time."

During World War II Clark Poling served as a chaplain on the troop ship, *Dorchester.* On a dark night while the ship was in the mid-Atlantic, a submarine torpedoed the ship, and it began to sink. Clark, along with two Catholic chaplains and a Jewish chaplain, took off their life belts and gave them to others. As the lifeboats shoved off, they knelt in prayer on the deck of the ship. There on the deck of a sinking ship, Poling and three other chaplains gave their answer to the seminary class question. "Our faith," Lyons observed, "is tested, not in textbooks or in words, but when lives are committed."[11]

The way lies before us. Jesus has called us to be men and women of His way. For some it requires the ultimate sacrifice, a life laid down like our Lord. It is a call to a giving life, a sacrificing life. Having received so much from a God who loves so greatly, we, too, are constrained to walk in that self-giving Way. Isaac Watts has written these words of thanksgiving for such amazing love.

> When I survey the wondrous cross,
> On which the Prince of glory died,
> My richest gain I count but loss,
> And pour contempt on all my pride.

> Were the whole realm of nature mine,
> That were a present far too small;
> Love so amazing, so divine,
> Demands my soul, my life, my all.[12]

Notes

1. Some of these references may be found in Romans 14:14, 1 Corinthians 7:10, 9:14; 1 Thessalonians 4:15f; 1 Timothy 5:8.

2. Keith Miller, *Habitations of Dragons* (Waco, Tex.: Word Books, 1970), pp. 88-89.

3. Quoted in David Dunn, *Try Giving Yourself Away* (Englewood Cliffs, N.J.: Prentice-Hall, Inc., 1956), p. 84.

4. Ibid, p. 85.

5. Raymond E. Balcomb, *Stir What You've Got!* (Nashville: Abingdon Press, 1968), pp. 50-51.

6. George W. Truett, *Some Vital Questions* (Grand Rapids, Mich.: Wm. B. Eerdmans, Co., 1946), p. 35.

7. Quoted in Ralph W. Sockman, *The Pulpit,* (May, 1950), p. 108.

8. Walter Rauschenbusch, *A Theology for the Social Gospel* (N. Y.: The Macmillan Co., 1917). p. 48.

9. Frederick W. Robertson. *Sermons Preached at Brighton* (New York: Harper & Brothers, n.d.), p. 195.

10. William Owen Carver. *The Acts of the Apostles* (Nashville: Sunday School Board of the SBC, 1916), p. 207.

11. Jesse Lyons, "These Triumphant Themes." Unpublished sermon delivered at Riverside Church, New York City, on August 24, 1975.

12. Isaac Watts, "When I Survey the Wondrous Cross," *Baptist Hymnal* (Nashville: Convention Press, 1975), p. 111.